G000241361

THERE'S NO PLACE

THE AMERICAN HOUSING CRISIS AND WHAT IT MEANS FOR THE UK

by Glyn Robbins

Red Roof publishes books about housing. We're particularly keen on stories of grassroots struggles for housing justice. If you've got an idea for a book, please get in touch.
Red Roof Publishing
c/o 20 Moravian Street, London E2 0NJ
redroofpublishing1@gmail.com

Design: Smith+Bell info@smithplusbell.com
Print: The Russell Press info@russellpress.com

Front cover:
Museum Square
protest in DC.
Back cover:
Abandoned Jersey
City public housing.

New Orleans,
Lower 9th.

"Buy land! They're not making it any more"
Mark Twain

"I hoped it was a time bomb under the bullshit of capitalism, this pseudo life that sought to touch the clouds by standing on top of a refrigerator, waving a paid-up mortgage at the moon, victorious at last!"
Arthur Miller on Death of a Salesman

"There's no place like home"
Dorothy Gale in The Wizard of Oz

Contents

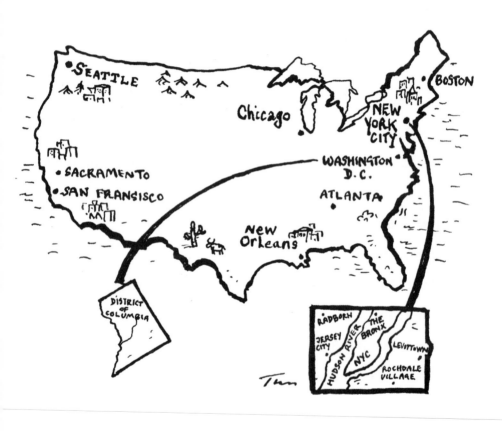

Cities visited
during field
research,
May/June
2015.

Author's note

The field research for this book was carried out in May/June 2015 and written up over the following six months. A lot's changed since then! Although I refer to it in the text, the political ascendancies of Messrs Corbyn, Sanders and Trump (and Trump's election as president!) were almost unimaginable back then.

Likewise, I write about the UK's Housing and Planning Act before a successful campaign of opposition compelled Theresa May's government to back-track on significant parts of the legislation. However, the Act became law on 12th May 2016. In my view, it's the culmination of policies driving the convergence of trans-Atlantic housing policy and remains a significant threat until or unless it's repealed.

One of the reasons for government concessions on the Act was the fall-out from the referendum in June 2016 which voted for the UK to leave the European Union. "Brexit" casts a long shadow over the future of the UK, including the socio-economic and political forces which underpin the commodification of housing in the US and UK.

It's too early to assess the full implications for US housing policy of Donald Trump becoming President, or how this might affect the UK, but the early signs are not good. Ben Carson has been appointed Secretary for the Department of Housing and Urban Development (HUD). Carson has no relevant experience, but has expressed his hostility to non-market housing. The new administration is looking to reduce the annual HUD budget by $6 billion (13 per cent), meaning severe cuts to investment and community development programmes.[1]

---

[1] "Trump budget asks for $6 billion in HUD cuts, drops development grants", *Washington Post*, 16th March 2017.

So everything's changed – but everything stays the same. There are still millions of British and American people whose lives are blighted by the catastrophic failure of their governments to administer a basic social and human need. Indeed, the swipes against the status quo of the last 18 months were, I think, strongly linked to the pent-up anger and frustration caused by our mutually dysfunctional housing systems. The primary aim of this book is to give voice to some of the people most affected by the US housing crisis and link their experience to those of people in the UK. Inevitably, since I met them, some of their stories have moved on and where possible, I have provided a brief update. The underlying social injustice implicit in our housing malaise remains the same.

I owe a debt of gratitude to the many people I met and interviewed during my research trip. Their real names appear throughout the text (except where anonymity was requested). These are only brief extracts from the time and insight they gave me. In 2017, in the aftermath of a Presidential election some saw as confirmation of the worst aspects of America, I cherish those encounters as a reminder of the great generosity of spirit I've always found in the US.

I argue that US and UK housing have a great deal in common, but that doesn't include spelling and terminology! In general, I have used standard English spelling, with apologies to American readers. I also use the English dating system (day followed by month). Where I use unfamiliar titles or acronyms, I initially spell them out and provide an explanation. There's also a list of abbreviations (page vi).

I tend to use the terms 'UK' for United Kingdom and 'US' for the United States of America, partly for brevity, but also to avoid more contentious names.

When I refer to the State as the seat of national government, I use capitals, but when referring to an individual state within the US, it will be in lower case.

I also have an aversion to the word "race" to describe differences between people who may have different skin colours and cultural backgrounds, but are actually part of the same race. I prefer ethnicity. I also dislike the terms "black" and "white" – we're all a mixture of both these things and more – but I use them as they are used in common parlance.

A particular clarification is needed about types of non-market, municipally-owned rented housing. Unless otherwise stated, I am specific about council housing in the UK and its nearest equivalent in the US, public housing. I avoid the terms social and affordable housing because they have become part of a deliberate manipulation of language which is discussed in the text.

I use the Harvard system of referencing in footnotes. There's a list of suggested further reading at the end of the book.

Acknowledgments

I'm particularly grateful to Larry Vale for reading an early draft and making detailed and constructive comments: also to Rob Chaskin and Jay Arena for their help with the Chicago and New Orleans chapters respectively.

Andy Smith has been more comrade than designer, likewise Tim Sanders who drew the map and Carol Williams who proof-read.

Thanks to Ken Loach, Marj Mayo, Truus Jansen, Michael Kane and Suz Muna for their kind words and encouragement.

I'd also like to thank the residents of the Quaker Court estate in Islington who both pay my wages and remind me of the true value of council housing. Numerous people helped me with my research in the US. Many of them are mentioned in the text, but for any who aren't, thank you.

Some of the issues in the book have reminded me of the supreme importance of friends and family. I can't thank you enough for what you give me (including the new Syrian branch of my family).

My daughters, granddaughter and departed son make me more proud than I can say. This book is dedicated to them and the memory of Alan Walter, Bob Rigby and my dad, George Robbins, – all fighters for housing justice in their own ways – and to those following in their footsteps.

Finally and always, Eileen Short has improved my life (and my writing), beyond measure. Mistakes in both remain mine.

Terms and abbreviations

AMI	Area Median Income: statistic often used in the US to calculate rent levels. Rents for non-market housing are commonly related to income in the US and are becoming more so in the UK.
CDC	Community Development Corporation: Non-profit organisations working in low-income areas of the US.
CNI	Choice Neighbourhood Initiative: US government-backed programme for revitalising public housing.
DCH	Defend Council Housing: UK-based, non-party political campaign organisation dedicated to defending and promoting council housing.
Garden Cities	A concept of urban development based on building planned communities outside of city centres with a balanced provision of homes, employment and amenities.
HA	Housing Association: housing provider in the UK, now officially known as "Private Registered Providers".
HB	Housing Benefit: means-tested rent subsidy in the UK available to tenants, but subject to increasing restrictions.
HUD	Department of Housing and Urban Development: US government department responsible for supervising public housing and other non-market housing programmes.
HOPE VI	Homeownership Opportunities for People Everywhere: HUD programme launched in 1992 aimed at replacing rented public housing with mixed tenure housing.
LIHTC	Low Income Housing Tax Credit
MIPIM	Le Marché International des Professionnels de L'Immobilier: convention of global property development industry that meets annually in Cannes, France and occasionally in other European cities.

NAHT	National Alliance of HUD Tenants: US-based, tenant-led campaign organisation representing low-income people living in non-market and subsidised rented housing.
NDC	New Deal for Communities: UK programme for regenerating council estates, launched by Labour government in 1998.
New Urbanism	An influential theory of urban design based on traditional housing design and street layouts.
NLIHC	National Low Income Housing Coalition: US-based advocacy and lobbying organisation.
PHA	Public Housing Authority: Municipal organisation responsible for administering US public housing.
RAD	Rental Assistance Demonstration: HUD programme aimed at attracting more funding to public housing, particularly from private sector.
REIT	Real Estate Investment Trust: financial product for speculative investment in housing.
Right to Buy	The Right to Buy (RTB) was introduced in 1980 by Margaret Thatcher's Conservative government. It gave UK council tenants the right to purchase their home, with a significant discount. Approximately 1.5 million homes have been sold. (RTB has now been suspended in parts of Wales and ended in Scotland.)
Section 8	The main form of means-tested rent subsidy available to US public and private tenants.
Stock Transfer	The UK transfer of former council estates to housing associations.
Third Sector	Organisations that claim to be in neither the public nor private sectors e.g. charities, "non-profits" and housing associations.

Introduction

My journey

I am fascinated by the relationship between UK and US housing (and America more generally) and have been for many years. I've also worked in housing since 1990 and been an active campaigner on housing issues. I've visited the US many times, had a brief period working as an intern for a public housing authority and have a long association with the National Alliance of HUD Tenants (NAHT), from whose members I have learned a great deal about the day-to-day struggle for decent homes in the US. Building on this, the primary source for this book was a six-week research visit to the US in May/June 2015. The itinerary for my journey was organised around meetings with a network of US housing activists, advocates and experts, with the aim of collecting stories and experiences from different places: Boston, the New York City area, Chicago, Seattle, San Francisco (and Sacramento), New Orleans, Atlanta and Washington DC.

The following chapters follow the order in which I visited these cities, so to some extent it is a travelogue. The stops on my journey weren't accidental. Each place has particular characteristics highlighting a different facet of the housing crisis. My aim is to describe these issues with reference to their comparators in the UK and build up an overall picture of how trans-Atlantic housing policy is converging around a pro-business consensus that intensifies housing need and social inequality. But it's important to recognise the limitations of my research. America is a vast, diverse country where local and regional differences create specific housing dynamics which can vary in a similar way that the housing situation varies in different parts of the UK. I acknowledge my fieldwork doesn't embrace the full range of the US housing experience. There are gaps (e.g. rural, Native-American, Deep South, Mid-West and small town housing) and the cities I did visit have differences within them that are sometimes greater than those between them. Similarly, I recognise that housing policy in the UK does not take account of the significant variations that exist in its different parts. There are some places where breaks have been applied to the privatisation engine. Also, I'm very conscious that the housing situation in London and the south-east of England is different to other areas of the country, but they are directly related. My argument is that the totality of US and UK housing policy and practice reveals distinct patterns that can be generalised because they stem from the same root and are having similar consequences for the people and communities at their mercy.

I also recognise the book covers a lot of ground – about 6,000 miles! Many of the subjects I refer to are worthy of far more detail, but I hope readers in both countries will recognise things from their own experience and discover things they may not have known about those of others. *There's No Place* is an attempt to make a small contribution towards raising awareness that those fighting for housing justice are facing a common foe.

My intention is to provide an accessible, demystified summary of the multi-layered and inter-woven issues that contribute towards an understanding of US/UK housing. I hope it will raise issues that are often hidden, even to those most affected by them. Most importantly, it tells the story of resistance and struggle at local level through the voices of those fighting to save their homes and communities. It's not a policy book aimed at an academic audience. Someone I met in Chicago said to me: "Please don't write a book for academics. The only people who read them are other academics." I've taken her words to heart.

My approach to this subject is not neutral. As well as my academic experience, I've had a wide range of housing jobs and I'm aware of the complexities and compromises that contribute towards policy formation and implementation. I don't argue that those responsible for these policies are "bad people". Likewise, while I am very critical of some of the things I've seen in the US, I am not anti-American. On the contrary, it's a place I love. However, this is a vital phase in the evolution of US/UK housing, urban and public policy, and a time to take sides. Mine is with those who believe another housing future – and world – is possible.

The 51st state of housing

In 1937, Richard Reiss, London County Council housing committee member and supporter of the Garden Cities movement, embarked on a tour of America. He concluded, "I saw enough to convince me that the United States has a vast housing problem."[2] I went to see what had changed, 78 years later. Like Reiss, I've worked in and campaigned on housing in the UK for many years. During that time, I've become increasingly conscious of the threads linking – and ultimately binding – the development of trans-Atlantic housing policy. This cross-fertilisation has, at times, appeared to define the differences between the two nations, with attitudes to housing reflecting wider cultural and political divergence. But it has now reached a critical point of convergence reflected in a common housing crisis. In both countries, plans are well advanced to detach housing, once and for all, from any semblance of public or non-profit provision and in the words of a right-wing UK housing academic, privatise the social rented stock and "allow market relations to develop".[3]

The housing histories of the US and UK are as intertwined as those of the two countries, with periods of closeness and distance

---

[2] Reiss R L (1937) *British and American Housing*, New York, National Public Housing Conference and archives of National Town and Country Planning Association.

[3] King P (1998) *Housing, Individuals and the State*, London, Routledge.

flowing from a common ancestry. Rugged individualism remains a powerful American motif, embodied in the ideal of private home ownership. This book describes some of the many hidden examples of a more collective approach to housing in the US, something more commonly associated with the UK. But, as the cultural, political and economic domination of private property becomes more ingrained, the British housing landscape increasingly resembles the American.

I argue there are five broad features of this shared US-UK housing experience:

1. Relentless government attacks on municipally-owned rented housing as part of a wider assault on public services.

2. The unchecked rise of private landlordism as part of a broader advancement of private sector, profit-seeking interests.

3. Growing corporate links between US and UK housing in the context of global speculative property investment.

4. Socially-divided cities characterised by displacement and denigration of poor and working class people and communities.

5. The ideological promotion of housing as a commodity, not a home.

One of the biggest contrasts in US-UK housing histories has been the extent of direct government intervention, most obviously illustrated by the UK's welfare state within which housing has been a significant component. While America's nearest equivalent, the 1930s New Deal, has left a lasting impression on US housing policy and although American governments have consistently intervened in housing provision, particularly through State funded private mortgages, the idea of "cradle to grave" State provision remains anathema to some deeply-held American belief systems. However, both nations are now at a crossroads in their attitudes to the scope of State involvement in housing and social welfare. UK governments have been chipping away at the welfare state for at least three decades, a process that began with selling-off council homes one by one and is now culminating in the wholesale privatisation not just of council housing, but a range of public services. Ironically, this moment arrives at a time when America is reappraising its attitude to Big Government. The partial extension of health care by the Obama administration has opened a wider debate about the wisdom of leaving vital services to the private sector.[4] Overall, however, this book argues that while some political alternatives may be gathering strength, the foreseeable housing futures of both nations are likely to be dictated by the whims and brutality of the market.

The fusion of US and UK housing policies and ideology are, for me, distilled in the Housing and Planning Act introduced by the Conservative government in autumn 2015 and passed into law on 12th May 2016. The sprawling legislation attracted significant criticism inside and outside parliament. It could catapult the UK towards the US housing model. Among its many measures, the Act sought to increase the rents of council tenants by linking them, for the first time, to income. Pay to Stay, as the government termed it, would see compulsory 15 per cent rent hikes for tenants seen as "high earners", though the income threshold for the increases was very low.[5] Beyond the numerous administrative problems associated with this move, it represents a fundamental breach with a founding principle of UK council housing: that it was designed to meet general need and available to anyone, irrespective of income. This universality was never part of US public housing and has contributed hugely to its character and problems. Similarly, the UK Act hopes to eliminate the permanent tenancy agreements that most council tenants have had since the 1980s. Thus the Tory government launched an assault on the qualities that have made council housing the most secure, affordable and popular form of rental housing in the UK, hoping to move it towards the conditional, marginal and transient condition of its US equivalent.

---

[4] This was confirmed by the difficulties President Trump had in his early attempts to abandon Obamacare.

[5] The combined income of £40,000 for the two top earners in a household in London, £31,000 outside London.

A very potted history of US/UK housing policy

The common origins of US and UK housing policy lie in attempts to alleviate the conditions of the 19th century industrial city. When utopian, charitable and philanthropic measures proved inadequate, the American and British establishments, under mounting pressure from organised labour, reluctantly accepted the need for action. However, from this early stage, differences emerged. In 1890, the Housing of the Working Classes Act enabled newly-created UK public authorities to clear and rebuild slums, paving the way for council housing. In 1891, the London County Council began demolishing the notorious Nichol rookery in Bethnal Green, east London.[6] Nine years later, the Prince of Wales opened the thousand-home Boundary Estate, the first of its type and scale in the world, still standing as a testament to its enduring quality and still in public ownership.

Faced with the same problem, the 1901 New York Tenement House Act concluded that improving the conduct of private developers and landlords, rather than replacing them, was the route to better conditions. As Peter Hall notes, American reformers feared that:

> ...public housing would mean a ponderous bureaucracy, political patronage (and) the discouragement of private capital...in comparison with Europe, it was to set the cause of public housing back for decades.[7]

From this fork in the road, both nations proceeded in a fashion reflecting their social characteristics. In the first quarter of the 20th century, the UK continued to build council housing against the backdrop of a strengthening labour movement and periodic rent strikes, which gave added impetus to creating alternatives to private landlordism. There were similar tenants' mobilisations in the US. But the country's labour movement struggled to recover from a vicious establishment attack in the aftermath of the Russian revolution. It was not until the crisis of the Great Depression that the

---

[6] Wise S (2008) *The Blackest Streets: The life and death of a Victorian slum*, London, Vintage Books.
[7] Hall P (1988) *Cities of Tomorrow*, (p39) Oxford, Blackwell.

US began to explore the possibilities of large-scale State intervention in housing.

The 1937 Wagner Stegall Housing Act might have been a turning point for US housing policy. The Act established legal and bureaucratic mechanisms by which 1.2 million homes would be built through State investment, administered by 3,000 local public housing authorities around the country. As in the UK, the shift towards municipal housing was part of a wider ideological movement that saw a decent home for all as central to a more enlightened society. However, in both countries, this idealism was tempered by compromise and pragmatism.

From the outset, US public housing was treated as ancillary to various other policy objectives, particularly job creation, but never as a rival to the supremacy of home ownership, which has enjoyed continuous financial, political and ideological support from US governments. The same is true of the UK, but for most of the 20th century, council housing was also part of the social and policy mainstream, providing a home to 30 per cent of the UK population by the end of the 1970s. Although public housing has assumed a significant place in some US cities, it has never housed more than five per cent of the national population. The reasons for this disparity are complex, but relate to significant cultural differences. For example, the totemic issue of state rights and its link to deeper concepts of independence and autonomy exert enormous political force in the US in a way that does not translate to the UK context. The balance of power between central and local US government plays out in a multitude of ways, including housing policy.

When the 1937 US Housing Act was introduced, it could only gain political endorsement on the basis that it would not impose Federal decree over local decision making, a tension that continues to shape US housing policy. From the beginning, there was also an absolute requirement that public housing would never be allowed to rival the private sector as the primary provider of new homes. There is something constant and fundamental in the relationship between America and property that needs to be recognised. The founding acts and principles of the nation were based on acquisition and enshrinement of land rights. These were exercised, most obviously and brutally, at the expense of Native Americans and established a commodification of land that has been ingrained in the European-American psyche.

But it would be wrong to regard US housing policy as monolithic. Since the 1930s there have been several changes in emphasis which, while not approaching the UK's post-war political consensus in favour of building council homes, demonstrate a recognition that government intervention is needed in the housing market. Like council housing, US public housing received a boost after World War Two, when the seeds of subsequent US housing policy were also sown. The initial imperative of finding homes for returning veterans led to the call, under the 1949 Housing Act, for 810,000 new public housing units (although only 84,000 were being built by 1951). The expansion of the municipal stock quickly gave way to the extension of government mortgage subsidies which became a far more embedded feature of US housing policy.

Initially made available to former servicemen, the scale of State support for private home ownership soon outstripped that for public housing. This spurred the development of the American suburbs and entrenched ethnic and skin colour divisions in US urban housing. Only white veterans were entitled to government-funded low-cost home ownership. African-Americans were effectively excluded from the expanding suburbs and consigned to neglected inner-city areas, often with appalling housing conditions. Housing has been an instrument of racism in many times and places, but has gained prolonged legitimacy in America. During my 2015 US trip, the Black Lives Matter campaign was a constant reminder of America's enduring and profound discomfort around race, something that housing policy continues to exacerbate.

Accumulating anxiety about America's urban crisis, periodically heightened by street unrest and rebellions, has directly influenced housing policy. Concerns, often expressed in moralistic, stigmatising and racialised terms, have been visited on public housing in particular. Since the 1960s, disinvestment and denigration has led to the sector being widely viewed as "the housing of last resort". A series of stereotypes have politically, physically and socially marginalised public housing and the people who live in it.

UK council housing has been the target of similar treatment since the 1980s. In both countries, the winding-down of direct State housing investment and provision has been accompanied by a variety of devices for advancing the role of the private sector, with significant trans-Atlantic mimicry. Proceeding from simplistic assumptions about design, both US and UK governments have used the camouflage of so-called partnership and regeneration, in the guise of policy initiatives such as HOPE VI in the US and New Deal for Communities in the UK, to achieve the privatisation of public and council housing respectively. This ideologically-driven assault has sought to create a more diverse range of housing providers and funding mechanisms, leading to increasingly complex and misleading definitions of affordable and social housing.

The development of a hybrid housing policy model (or muddle) has created at least 13 different programmes for the five million Americans who receive assistance with their housing costs. In the UK, the cumulative impact of the Right to Buy (creating multiple ownership patterns and private renting on council estates), the increasing role of housing associations, intermediate housing tenures (e.g. shared ownership) and the rise of private renting with its attendant sub-letting and multiple occupancy are creating a similarly complex housing picture.

While this book will focus on the growing resemblance between US and UK housing, there remain some fundamental differences. Perhaps the biggest of these is the extent of legal entitlements to housing. In the UK, certain categories of people – notably parents with children – can still present themselves as homeless to a local authority which then has a duty to house them (however inadequately). No such protection exists in the US. Although housing rights in the UK, particularly for the homeless, have been substantially reduced, the most vulnerable still have a safety net that doesn't exist across the Atlantic. Furthermore, a substantial part of access to low cost housing in the US is controlled and administered by a voucher system which enables eligible tenants to find housing in the public, or more likely, private rented sector. UK Housing Benefit (HB) is increasingly acting like a voucher system, but is part of a wider system of welfare benefits which doesn't exist in the US.[8] Similarly, although council and housing association housing sit within the wider context of the UK welfare state, they have never been considered "welfare housing" as their US equivalents often are. Access to public and other non-market housing in the US is rigorously controlled by means-testing, with rigid income limits and rent calculated as a proportion of income. Until the advent of the Housing and Planning Act in 2016, this was not the case in the UK.

Historically, the private rented sector has been far more sizeable in the US. This has changed dramatically in recent years. Private renting fell steadily in the UK during most of the 20th century – in inverse proportion to the rise of council housing – and settled at around eight per cent. That trend has now reversed. UK private renting has doubled in the last decade and is fast approaching US levels of 30 per cent, while social housing has fallen to 16 per cent, of which council homes make up only half.

This book will describe and explore a host of local issues illustrating that US and UK housing are morphing. The transnational force driving them together is the increasing economic reliance of both countries on the so called FIRE sector of finance, insurance and real estate (or property). This in turn relates to structural economic changes over the last four decades through the deregulation of global investment markets. The result is the increasing commodification of housing, now a speculative investment vehicle

---

[8] Current changes, particularly the introduction of Universal Credit, could significantly alter this.

for vast flows of global capital, the volatility of which brought repossession and homelessness for many in the sub-prime crisis of 2007-8. The grip of the international property machine has intensified since the great recession. Its primary targets are the high value areas of US and UK cities where over-heated housing markets are transforming, traumatising and trashing local neighbourhoods, particularly those with high concentrations of non-market housing.

The cross-fertilisation of US-UK housing was graphically demonstrated in October 2015 at a London convention of global property developers. The three-day MIPIM-UK[9] event billed itself as a "gathering of professionals looking to close deals in the UK property market". Sixteen US-based companies were represented at MIPIM-UK and among the subjects for discussion was The American Way. The US template of large-scale institutional investment in private renting was fawned over and illustrated in the conference brochure by a picture of the road to a house paved with dollar bills. The event detailed plans of several big US companies to expand into the UK, including Greystar – one of the biggest corporate private landlords in the US with 425,000 homes. Greystar opened its UK portfolio by acquiring 22,700 student apartments and has entered a partnership with Fizzy Living, a company that says it's "reinventing renting" in the UK. Fizzy Living is a subsidiary of Thames Valley Housing, a so-called non-profit housing association.

As flows of capital traverse the Atlantic, so too do attempts to resist the commodification of housing. On 14th October 2015, there was an international day of action, under the banner "our communities are not for sale", against Blackstone, the US-based private equity company. Blackstone has bought thousands of cut-price homes in America and Europe since the 2007-8 crash. Blackstone was also implicated in the collapse of the UK Southern Cross care homes chain in 2011, leading even the right-wing *Daily Mail* newspaper to describe the company as "sharks".[10]

---

[9] 'Marche International des Professionnels de L'Immobilier'.
[10] "£1 billion gamble of the care home sharks revealed", *Daily Mail*, 4th June 2011.

1

Boston – The British are coming!

Introduction

My journey began, appropriately, in Boston, where the strange idea of America really got started. The city steeped in rebellion is a place where the writ of the neoliberal consensus does not always run smoothly. But some of the key forces driving the housing crisis are much in evidence. Boston's waterfront setting and historic identity have stimulated the type of over-development of private apartments that has disfigured the landscape of most US and UK cities, while deepening social inequality.

The tourist-traps of revolution and nationhood are centred on areas where, in the early 1960s, sociologist Herbert Gans prophesised the displacement of working class communities from the inner-city. In his 1962 critique of urban renewal projects, Gans captures the diverse cultural and economic character of the "urban village" and its eclectic mix of uses and people.[11] Ironically, these qualities are used today as marketing slogans in government-sponsored property development campaigns and are fuelling another wave of displacement in Boston and beyond. In particular, the quasi-mystical concept of mixed communities have been used as a device for the destruction of public housing, a manoeuvre that had one of its first deployments in Boston, but has since become commonplace on both sides of the Atlantic.

In 1984, the 1,500-home Columbia Point public housing site, in the south of the city, was handed over to a private property company. This was a response to a cycle of decline, neglect and mismanagement that culminated in three-quarters of the homes standing empty. A private developer embarked on what has become a familiar process of remodelling and rebranding. The number of homes was reduced by 300 and 17 per cent of former residents were displaced in the early phases of the redevelopment.[12] Responding to public housing tenants' desires to live in a visually more conven-

---

[11] Gans H (1962) *The Urban Villages: Group and Class in the Life of Italian-Americans*, New York, The Free Press.

[12] "Columbia Point gives way to upscale Harbour Point", *Boston Globe*, 13th July 2015.

tional neighbourhood, and to commercial interests, 1950s multi-storey apartment blocks were demolished and replaced with low-rise blocks and town-houses adorned with clapboard and picket fences, built along traditional streets and pavements. Life-style rules were introduced in an attempt to control access and resident behaviour. Columbia Point was renamed Harbour Point and two-thirds of the new homes were for market sale or rent. This is the basic model for all the many regeneration projects at public and council housing sites since (although the city of Boston has been less zealous in pursuing this policy than some others). The seductive rhetoric of mixed communities has pervaded US and UK policy for two decades. Received wisdom maintains that deliberately combining different types of people, uses and activities produces an alchemistic blend that makes cities better. As Professor Paul Cheshire has argued,[13] there is no evidence to support the benefits of these "faith-based displacement activities", beyond anecdotal references to the kind of lamented urbanity celebrated by Jane Jacobs.[14] Other academic research has found that, far from nurturing social interaction, super-imposed mix actually reinforces socio-economic divisions.[15] However, since the HOPE VI initiative of the early 1990s – renamed by public housing tenants as "Homeless Opportunities for People Everywhere" – mixed income communities have been the engine of change and displacement in US public housing.

The contested terrain of public housing is only one aspect of Boston's volatile housing picture. From 19th century philanthropy to 21st century gentrification, the city presents examples of many of the issues that mark the shared US-UK passage to housing crisis.

---

[13] Cheshire P (2009) *Policies for mixed communities: faith based displacement activity?* in International Regional Science Review, Vol. 32 no. 3, pp 343 – 375.

[14] Jane Jacobs was a Boston US-Canadian urban theorist best known for her celebration of traditional cityscapes.

[15] Erin Michelle Graves' PhD thesis *Constructing Community* (MIT, 2008) and my unpublished PhD *Mixed Use Property Development and its Place in UK Urban Policy* (London Metropolitan University, 2013).

Charity begins at home

Boston's struggle for decent, genuinely affordable homes for those with low and moderate incomes has a long history and a direct link with the UK.[16] Victorian philanthropy laid the foundations for better housing on both sides of the Atlantic and Sidney Waterlow was one of its pioneers. Waterlow was born and raised in Finsbury in the City of London and apprenticed to his ambitious father's printing business. Waterlow's entrepreneurial success enabled him to join and finance the growing movement for social reform focussed on urban slums. In 1863 he founded the Improved Industrial Dwellings Society which eventually housed 30,000 Londoners.[17] After several trips to America, in 1886 Waterlow visited Boston and met Robert Treat Paine Jr. who had promoted housing reform in the US. Paine was a board member of the Boston Cooperative Building Company (BCBC), which in 1874 purchased ten acres of land in Dorchester, South Boston. Sixteen timber framed homes still stand (on Sidney and Waterlow streets) as testament to Paine's belief that decent, affordable housing could be brought to the American working classes. But by 1902 when the BCBC ceased trading, it had built only 62 more, an early indication of the limitations of the charitable model.

A more significant legacy exists in the Victorian mind-set that still pervades housing policy in the US and UK. Paternalist Waterlow and his peers believed working class people needed to be rescued from the failures of the housing market, but also from themselves. This was reflected in the authoritarian rules around access to and management of charitable – and eventually public – housing in both countries. Furthermore, Sidney Waterlow believed housing providers should sift, sort and separate potential residents according to their income. In discussing his approach to building homes Waterlow said:

---

[16] Vale L J (2007) *From the Puritans to the Projects*, Cambridge, Harvard University Press.
[17] Tarn J N (1973) *Five Per Cent Philanthropy: An account of housing in urban areas between 1840 and 1914*, Cambridge, Cambridge University Press.

> We must take the class as of various degrees; the upper, middle and lower of the labouring classes; it could not have been right to build down to the lowest class...we have rather tried to build for the best class, and by lifting them up to leave more room for the second and third who are below them.[18]

This thinking has its enduring equivalent in the idea of mixed income housing that now dominates US and UK housing policy. As at Columbia Point, a host of strategies are used to try to replace public housing, from neo-traditional architecture (timber framed homes, picket fences etc.) to the rebranding of places with bucolic names. However, while some aspects of the stigma visited on tenants may have been ameliorated by these changes, they have been replaced with others. A more pleasant environment for some has been accompanied by exclusion for others. In their detailed examination of mixed income initiatives in Chicago, Chaskin and Joseph conclude "these new communities expose poor people – and particularly relocated public housing residents – to different kinds of disadvantage and have generated new forms of exclusion".[19] Former public housing tenants admitted to mixed income sites have faced stringent vetting, authoritarian codes of behaviour and prejudice. The underlying philosophy remains the same as Sidney Waterlow's in the 19th century: an attempt to stratify access to non-market housing according to income and other social characteristics. The net effect is to institutionalise an even older ideology – the undeserving poor. For the unable, unlucky or unwilling, finding decent quality, genuinely affordable and secure housing in Boston, like other cities, has become a life-defining search.

---

[18] Evidence to the 1885 Royal Commission on the Housing of the Working Classes, (p425, para. 11.959), 13th June 1884.
[19] R J Cheaskin and M L Joseph (2015) *Integrating the Inner City: The Promise and Perils of Mixed-Income Public Housing Transformation*, (p224) Chicago, University of Chicago Press.

Boston Housing Authority – "catalysts for transformation"

One invaluable source of housing outside Boston's increasingly unaffordable private market is the Boston Housing Authority (BHA), which belies the ideologically-constructed image of public housing as marginalised and peripheral. One in ten Bostonians (58,000 people) live in BHA housing, rising to one in six in some areas (although an increasing proportion are now recipients of vouchers to rent in the private sector, rather than permanent homes). There's a significant concentration of BHA sites in South Boston, the historic Irish enclave where the current BHA executive director, Bill McGonagle, was himself brought up in public housing. Created due to determined political action by the Irish-Americans of South Boston, the city's oldest public housing is the Mary Ellen McCormack development, where Mr McGonagle was a child. He recalls:

> I was born and raised at Mary Ellen McCormack with my five brothers and sisters. My mom was a homemaker and my dad was a bus driver. I was an altar boy at St. Monica's Church right up the street. Me and my two brothers spent our summers on Carson Beach. Mary Ellen is a place I have extraordinarily fond memories of: memories I will carry with me for as long as I live. [20]

Mary Ellen McCormack was built in 1938, part of the first New Deal generation of US public housing. In Boston as elsewhere in the US, housing is never far from the politics of ethnicity and exclusion.[21] Early public housing was presented as a salvation for poor but respectable white slum dwellers. Access was restricted both by skin colour and ability to pay significantly higher rents. A similar process accompanied the early days of UK council housing.

From the outset, urban regeneration projects, bringing higher rents, restrictive tenancies and the inevitability of people resettling elsewhere during prolonged redevelopment, meant that displace-

---

[20] Email to the author, 27th May 2015.
[21] Vale L J (2002) *Reclaiming Public Housing: A half century of struggle in three public neighbourhoods*, Cambridge, Harvard University Press.

Mary Ellen McCormack, Boston public housing.

ment was deliberate. Eight decades later, these dynamics remain at play in the creation of the "Mixed Income Communities" replacing public housing in Boston and beyond.

Concetta Paul is proud to be a BHA tenant and says it's the only way she could afford to live in the city and send her son to college. She lives in a BHA block at West Broadway, South Boston where the signs of neglect and disinvestment – battered doorways, dimly-lit and littered corridors – are immediately apparent. Concetta looks with some wistfulness at the new mixed income homes opposite hers, where a private management company maintains the lawns and administers the income-entry requirements of $39,401 for a two-bedroom, four-person apartment. The Area Median Income (AMI) for Boston is $70,000, but the poorest 20 per cent of Bostonians, including Concetta and many other public housing tenants, have income below $15,000.

Boston public housing, old and new.

As she shows me around her neighbourhood, Concetta advises me to take photos of the public housing "because it won't be there the next time you come". She takes me to what's left of the 1940s, brick built Old Colony BHA site, which has already undergone partial redevelopment using the mixed income communities blueprint. It's in a place that's the stuff of property developer dreams. You can imagine the sales blurb: "Come to vibrant, historic South Boston and enjoy spectacular water-front views from your

luxury private condo – a five minute walk from Carson Beach, a 20 minute walk to your downtown office. You can have it all!" and the subtext: "Don't worry about those low-income families who used to live here. We've got rid of most of them".

BHA denies deliberately displacing its tenants and it has a record of trying to preserve low-income housing, albeit through the complex range of alternatives that are a feature of the US system. The Rental Assistance Demonstration (RAD) is the latest euphemistically-named federal government initiative aimed at paring away another layer of public housing by allowing tenants to be charged market rents. BHA has identified RAD as an "opportunity" to confront the "serious challenges" of cuts in funding, creating an annual operating deficit of $6.8 million and a cumulative repairs backlog of $500 million. The authority is also attempting to attract private sector investment and owners for its housing. In spring 2015, BHA invited expressions of interest from "qualified real estate development firms to optimise the value of BHA sites in high-market neighbourhoods, as a means to preserve or expand existing affordable units". Given the impoverishment of most existing public housing tenants, the possibility of charging higher rents in high market neighbourhoods can only mean attracting residents with more money than Concetta Paul.

Over there, over here

BHA portrays the involvement of the private sector as benign, or as the only way of attracting the money needed to improve public housing. This Faustian pact is very familiar to UK council tenants. Since the 1980s, successive British governments have used a variety of schemes to lever private finance into housing as an alternative to direct public investment.[22] These attempts intensified under the post-1997 New Labour government, which stated its intention of transferring 200,000 council homes a year to new owners as part of a Decent Homes policy. A long series of local campaigns for and against these transfers ensued, with each camp arguing the benefits and risks of removing entire estates from public ownership (unlike the RAD initiative, stock transfer usually has to be mandated by a ballot of affected tenants). Some of these arguments were quite difficult, particularly where they juxtaposed possible long-term adverse consequences with the offer of short-term improvements

---

[22] Pawson H and Mullins D (2010) *After Council Housing: Britain's New Social Landlords*, Basingstoke, Palgrave Macmillan.

to tenants' homes. However, a decade later the UK experience provides some warnings to the US.

An overall assessment of wholesale council house privatisation is difficult because the issues played out at local, even individual, level. But some key conclusions are clear. One of the main arguments of advocates for involving the private sector was that tenants' interests and public assets would be protected by the non-profit and charitable housing associations (HAs) who would become the new social landlords. (A similar conceit is being used for RAD.) Even at the time, this betrayed a fundamental misunderstanding (or deliberate misrepresentation) of the nature of HAs, which are legally constituted as private businesses, governed by unelected Boards and have very limited public transparency or accountability. These facts have become more pertinent since. HAs, now renamed Private Registered Providers, acquired 1.2 million former council homes between 1998 and 2008 and their activities have become increasingly commercialised. Some commentators have described HAs as the "true villains" of the housing crisis.[23] This is inaccurate and unfair. But their activities have certainly deviated significantly from the social function they were established to fulfil. This shift was starkly exposed when one of the biggest HAs, Genesis, announced it was no longer going to build affordable homes for people on low incomes. In the words of their Chief Executive "We are not able, or being asked, to provide affordable and social rented accommodation to people who should be looking to the market to solve their own problems."[24]

This statement confirmed the dramatic changing emphasis of HA activities. In 2010-11, approximately 60 per cent of the homes they built in England were for social rent (i.e. substantially below the market rate). By 2014-15 that proportion had fallen to six per cent. The others were either for shared ownership or the so-called

---

[23] Ross Clark "Why housing associations are the true villains of the property crisis", *The Spectator*, 25th July 2015.
[24] "Changing Focus", *Inside Housing*, 30th July 2015.

Affordable Rents that are up to 80 per cent of the market level.[25] This move away from genuine affordable rented housing will intensify under the Housing and Planning Act 2016 and subsequent Housing White Paper[26] which further deregulate HAs, fulfilling the wishes of a right-wing think tank which envisages them as organisations suitable for institutional private investment.[27]

The experience of tenants who transferred to a housing association has been varied and, again, subject to local circumstances (and significantly under-researched). It would be wrong to say that every aspect of stock-transfer has been bad.[28] Many homes and estates did receive needed physical and environmental improvements, but these have been bought at a significant social and financial cost. As well as losing a directly accountable landlord and important legal protections from eviction, in numerous cases tenants have seen their estates redeveloped with an injection of private housing on a scale that has fundamentally altered the character of their communities.[29] In both the US and UK, one of the key justifications for transferring publicly-owned housing to the private sector has been that this is the most cost-effective – indeed the only – way to pay for necessary repairs and improvements. Some have argued this is a false economy. In 2003, the UK's National Audit Office estimated that improving council housing via stock transfer would cost £1,300 per home more than direct public investment.[30] In both the US and UK, housing finance is governed by byzantine rules and accountancy conventions which deliberately frustrate attempts to invest in non-market housing. Calling for a level playing field for housing investment, in 2009 a group of MPs argued, "If govern-

---

[25] "RPs complete 51,956 new homes in final year of AHP" *Social Housing*, 4th September 2015.

[26] DCLG (2017) *Fixing Our Broken Housing Market*, London, HMSO.

[27] Policy Exchange *Freeing Housing Associations: Better financing, more homes* (2014).

[28] Joseph Rowntree Foundation, *The Impacts of Housing Stock Transfers in Urban Britain* (2009).

[29] Watt P (2009) *Housing Stock Transfers, Regeneration and State-Led Gentrification in London* in Urban Policy and Research, Vol. 27, no. 3 pp 229 – 242.

[30] NAO, *Improving Social Housing Through Transfer*, March 2003.

ment is prepared to pour billions into funding privatisation through stock transfer, then there is no financial reason why they cannot redirect those resources into council housing."[31]

Boston attempts to "optimise the value of BHA sites" also has a familiar ring to UK ears. In April 2014 Eric Pickles, the minister with ultimate responsibility for housing in the post-2010 Coalition government, launched a report from property consultants Savills. In it, Pickles described London council estates as "brownfield sites" suitable for "optimal, wholesale regeneration" based on private investment able to "create value in land" and thus increase the supply, density and quality of housing in urban areas. The 2016 Housing and Planning Act is designed to accelerate the redefinition of council estates, changing them from socially diverse, essentially working class communities, into places ripe for transnational property investment.

Churchill Gardens in Pimlico, west London, is a classic example of the places Pickles and the corporate development industry have in mind. The pioneering 30-acre, 1,600 home estate on the banks of the River Thames was built by a Conservative local authority in the post-war period when council housing was seen as a vital part of a fairer, more peaceful, society. Replacing bomb-damaged terraced streets, Churchill Gardens was part of an integrated plan for local services based on public investment and public ownership. Some of the best architects of the time worked on the design, prioritising light-filled, spacious homes alongside a community centre, landscaped gardens, schools, shops and one of the first combined heat and power energy systems in the UK.

Today, Churchill Gardens is located in one of the most expensive property markets in Britain, where multi-million pound house prices are the norm. As in Boston, a triad of policy makers, politicians and property developers are seeing places like Churchill

---

[31] House of Commons Council Housing Group, *Council Housing: Time to Invest – fair funding, investment and building council housing* (2009).

Gardens, with their desirable locations and proximity to city centres, as prime sites for redevelopment, privatisation and profiteering. In the words of Mary Farrell, a long-time Churchill Gardens resident:

> When they see Churchill Gardens, they see money. They don't see a community where people know each other and look out for one another. It's happening everywhere. There are at least 50 council estates around London under threat of demolition. It's social cleansing. But residents are getting organised and we're going to fight to save our homes.

The distinguishing feature of council housing, like US public housing, is that it is largely insulated from the volatility and profit-making potential of the speculative property market. This is a challenge to those seeking the unrestricted operation of market relations in housing. The fact that Churchill Gardens, like some public housing in Boston and other US cities, is occupying tracts of valuable land infuriates them, but also presents a problem: people with secure tenancies live there! Using violence to remove tenants is, in general, politically awkward, so a narrative of justification is constructed whereby coerced displacement is disguised as a series of pragmatic, policy-induced choices. This process has been at work, on both sides of the Atlantic, for many years. It could be approaching its zenith.

BHA says there is no alternative but to partly or wholly privatise public housing. But as Michael Kane, a veteran Boston housing campaigner argues, this is based on a historic layering of political decisions. Michael relates a conversation with a former senior executive at the US department of Housing and Urban Development (HUD) who admitted that failing to invest in public housing is a false economy. The costs of subsidies to developers, rehousing former tenants and additional welfare benefit payments to those compelled to move by privatising redevelopment projects far exceed the money needed to bring BHA and other public housing up to a decent standard. But as the HUD officer said to Michael Kane, rational policy arguments for investment in non-market housing flounder against what politicians see as the political impotence of the people who live in it.

Demonisation and Privatisation

A vital accompaniment to the attempted destruction of US public and UK council housing has been a deliberate and prolonged campaign of denigration and stigmatisation. In the US (and to a lesser extent the UK) this process has been heavily inscribed with racism. The depiction of The Projects (i.e. US public housing sites) as violent and dangerous has been embedded in popular culture. As a recent book dispelling public housing myths comments:

> [For decades] reporters in the United States have developed a series of persistently demeaning and dehumanising public housing memes and tropes. Mostly middle-class reporters find public housing convenient shorthand for all urban poverty, government malfeasance, rampant criminality and dependence.[32]

In the UK, as Owen Jones has observed, "prejudices about poverty and unemployment converge in the image of the council estate."[33] Media images of places where only the most desperate live have been reinforced by policies that have deliberately weakened the economic base of non-market housing and the people who live in it. Some attempts have been made to challenge the negative stereotypes that accompany this vicious cycle. In the UK, the Defend Council Housing (DCH) campaign has argued for 20 years that council housing pays for itself in both economic and social terms. In the US in 2013, a multi-media PR campaign urged people to "Rethink Housing" by highlighting personal success stories of public housing tenants and the sector's positive role in building community stability.

---

[32] Dagen Bloom N, Umbach F and Vale L J (eds) (2015) *Public Housing Myths: Perception, reality and social policy* (p11), Ithaca, Cornell University Press.
[33] Jones O (2011) *Chavs: The demonization of the working class* (p206) London, Verso.

In both countries, campaigners draw attention to the fact that public/council housing offers lower rents, more security of tenure and better conditions than are available to most in the private rented sector. Perhaps because of this, the most telling assessment of public/council housing is that "the only people who like it are the people who live there". As the housing crisis deepens on both sides of the Atlantic, the number of people who would *like* to live there is increasing rapidly.

Leaving it to the market (and the Games)

Despite growing need, the political case for more government spending on genuinely affordable, secure housing has not been won. The argument that tenants form a weak political constituency may have some truth in the US – though less so in the UK, where they have historically had more power – but raises wider issues about the socio-economic and ideological role of housing in American and British society. Some of these concerns are illustrated by Boston's 15-year housing plan, unveiled by Mayor Marty Walsh in October 2014. Like many politicians, Mayor Walsh knows there's a huge housing problem, but his remedies rely on the same formula that's been responsible for causing it. Detailed analysis by the Mayor's office of the scale of housing demand, particularly from people on low and medium income, acknowledges the cost of housing in Boston is pricing people out of the city. But the Mayor's plan rests heavily on a market-driven approach to supply the 53,000 homes his administration says the city needs by 2030. The inflated price of housing is acting as a device for social engineering in Boston, as in many other US and UK cities. In 2013 – 2014, a family with income of $80,000 could only afford 4.7 per cent of homes that came on the market in South Boston. Given this, it's no surprise that in this traditionally working class area, the number of residents earning over $100,000 has increased by 24 per cent during the past decade.[34]

---

[34] "Walsh wants 53,000 more housing units in Boston by 2020", *Boston Globe*, 9th October 2014.

Boston's demographic shift is being actively fed by the kind of boosterist rhetoric synonymous with cities around the world seeking to market themselves as "World Class". This phoney competition exists only in the minds of politicians, PR consultants and municipal functionaries. It means nothing to citizens except that they pay for the marketing strategies and the consequences of growth – seemingly the only mark of a city's success. Until late July 2015, Boston was pursuing the Olympics, the ultimate symbol of fantasised urban lifestyles. Since 1992, when the Games were held in Barcelona, the Olympics have been presented as a magic spell for urban regeneration. A significant amount of scholarly research has questioned the actual social and economic benefits of mega-sports events. The experience of people living in Atlanta, Beijing, Rio de Janeiro and other Olympic cities testify to a history of displacement and ever-escalating costs. Despite this, Mayor Walsh and his backers, including local labour unions, attempted to persuade Bostonians of the multiple benefits of hosting the 2024 Olympics, in language familiar to people living in London prior to the 2012 Games:

> Going for the Olympics allows us to market the city around the world in 110 different countries, and constantly be on the world news and the world stage for the next two years. While we're in that conversation, we'll see tremendous benefits, including an increase in tourism [and] interest in our city by foreign investors.[35]

The disconnection between the Olympic hype and the reality of most peoples' lives was exposed when Boston's bid was unceremoniously dropped because its blank cheque funding requirement could not command the support of most people in the city.[36] Campaigners described the Games as "fool's gold" and contested the assumed contribution to meeting housing need:

---

[35] Interview with *Boston Curbed* website, 25th March 2015.
[36] In a further sign that reality may be pricking the Olympic bubble, in November 2015, the people of Hamburg also rejected the opportunity to host the Games.

The London Olympic Village was converted into 2,818 new housing units. Mayor Marty Walsh recently announced that Boston needs 53,000 new housing units. You could build a new Olympic Village each year from now until 2030 and you would still fall short of Boston's housing needs. Hosting an Olympic Games will distract from achieving Mayor Walsh's important goal of providing housing for all Bostonians. [37]

Housing and Right to the City

As Boston goes back to the housing drawing-board, there's a place in the city that provides an example of a more sustainable solution than the ephemera of sports events and property speculation. In April 1968, following the assassination of Martin Luther King Jr, the South End neighbourhood, like many across America, erupted in anger.[38] A focus of demands for social and housing justice was a vacant plot where the Boston Redevelopment Agency (BRA) planned a multi-storey car park as part of its sweeping, car-oriented urban renewal plan. Led by Mel King, a community campaigner still active five decades later, the site was occupied by protestors. They pitched tents and demanded an end to displacement and more affordable housing instead of road building. In a reminder of the kind of attritional time-scales of successful housing campaigns, 15 years later agreement was reached for the development of Tent City, a 269-home collection of apartments and townhouses opposite Back Bay station in the heart of Boston. Seventy-five per cent of these were – and remain – for people on low and medium incomes. Speaking in May 2015 at a public meeting I attended at Tent City under the title *Is there a future for public housing?*, Mel King linked housing struggles to a wider set of social justice issues:

---

[37] www.nobostonolympics.org/myths
[38] These were somewhat contained after the singer James Brown held a concert in the city in which he issued a "call for calm".

There's a way you define what City Life is:[39] access to housing that's affordable and enables people to enjoy life in the city. A house is a physical structure. A home is a spiritual, social, loving structure. I was at college in South Carolina when my folks sent me a newspaper with a headline saying that the South End was a slum. I grew up in this neighbourhood. It was one of the best. Thirty-two different ethnic, racial cultures. You name a food from anywhere in the world, we had it here. We had Armenian grocery stores, Italian bakeries, Jewish delis. We had great music. So I understood what community was.

The fact that we didn't have much money didn't mean we couldn't have rich lives and relationships. I came back from college to do my Masters degree in teaching. My tuition fees were $108 [laughter from audience], but at those levels working class people were able to afford higher education without mountains of debt. There's no reason why it couldn't happen now. Education goes hand in hand with why we're in this room – to oppose policies and practices based on greed, not need.

We decided to take on the Boston Redevelopment Authority (BRA) in 1968 because we'd seen what went on in the West End of the City. We said "we can't let that happen here". We put a picket line around this site. We insisted that decisions about the future of the area had to be taken by the people who lived here. We built a broad coalition. Almost all of the housing that got built here came out of that process. But we were willing to go to jail.

One of the most important books I've read is *The Right of Revolution*. This country was founded on that idea. I have a right because I'm somebody. I am deserving. I'm not going to allow someone to just do something that devalues who I am. We mustn't allow ourselves to be devalued and if they can just move us out, they're devaluing us. We have to stand up to make sure that it's not going to happen.

So you need to get a cross-section of people together, understand what the law says and sometimes get your elected officials to change the law.

---

[39] City Life is a Boston housing campaign organisation.

Glyn and Mel King.

But you can never rest on your laurels. You have to stay on top of the case otherwise they'll find a way to circumvent promises. We had an agreement at another central Boston site [Copley Place] for 25 per cent affordable housing, but the mayor tried to water it down to 15 per cent and move it off site. The politicians did a deal with the developers.

But I also remember – and it brought tears to my eyes – when they were trying to introduce HOPE VI to the Cathedral public housing site and a man at one of the consultation meetings stood up and said "it's not going to happen". There was a fight and a few years later they came back with $8 million to fix up the place. There are thousands of other homes in Boston that have been protected and preserved for working class people. It's great that we're here at Tent City, but we have to continue the fight.

Tent City, Boston.

Cultural contrasts

Mel King's testimony has a universal quality, but also alludes to some of the important cultural differences between housing struggles in the US and UK. In 1835 Alexis de Tocqueville observed: "Americans of all ages, all stations of life and all types of disposition are forever forming associations." [40] A spirit of voluntarism remains one of the defining characteristics of American life, reflected in sports clubs, civic organisations and a profusion of housing campaigns not only in Boston but across the US. They've emerged from and exist in a significantly different political and ideological context to their UK counterparts. There are some important common threads, notably a shared interest in the ethos and practice of co-operativism. But the trajectory of reform and labour movements has produced very differ-

[40] De Tocqueville A (1835) *Democracy in America*, (p596), London, Penguin Books (2003 edition).

ent results, in particular a welfare state in the UK, the US equivalent of which was strangled at birth. A range of public services during much of the 20th century engendered a tradition of public service entitlement within the British working class that has never been shared by American workers, who have instead cultivated a self-reliance, creativity and energy sometimes absent in the UK. At a very crude level, this is illustrated when the time comes in a meeting for people to volunteer to do things. In the UK, people are prone to stare at their hands; Americans are likely to raise them!

There are many complex societal consequences of this cultural contrast. In the housing field they manifest themselves in the historic under-provision and marginal status of American public housing, but also in a sense of optimism amongst campaigners that better housing can be won. A mirror opposite pertains in the UK, where the steady erosion of State-funded housing has left a general feeling that the best is behind us. This is reflected in the many accounts of British housing lamenting the glories of a black-and-white housing age, leading to a decline often depicted in pathological, dystopian terms. For example, Lynsey Hanley's widely read and discussed *Estates*[41] presents a nostalgic image of council housing and then maps an inexorable (at least for Hanley) decline. Advocates for council housing frequently have to combat a repository of negative associations that have become common currency, particularly amongst those with a vested political or commercial interest.

US public housing has never approached the kind of widespread – in some places, almost universal – collective identity and experience shared by UK council tenants. Council housing, by its nature, instils a level of political engagement and participation, one of the reasons why its enemies have worked so hard and long to destroy it. Council tenants have been described as "unique citizens"[42] because of their potential to exercise organisational and political

---

[41] Hanley L (2007) *Estates: an intimate history*, London, Granta Books.
[42] Grayson J (2009) *Looking at Tenant History: Different histories, different politics*, Leeds Tenants Federation.

strength capable of successfully challenging State policy, something that has been demonstrated once again during the campaign against the Housing and Planning Act. Conversely, there is also an argument that the provision of a wholesale range of public services, including council housing, led to a degree of passivity and inertia in the UK working class. Put over-simply, British people have expectations of State provision. Americans have very few.

This contrast assumes decreasing significance in the present context, of the dismantling of the post-war British welfare state. The proportion of council tenants has fallen from 30 per cent of households in 1979 to eight per cent in 2015. But there remain differences in the struggle for decent housing on either side of the Atlantic. Mel King articulated one of them. The notion of housing as intrinsic to a wider set of rights, including the Right to the City, employs a lexicon still unfamiliar to British ears. Although Henri Lefebvre's *Le Droit a la Ville* has attracted debate in some academic and left-wing circles, it is not part of the UK campaign mainstream, where, until quite recently, these rights were assumed to be already won. They were never attained in America and in this fundamental sense US and UK housing campaigns start in a different place, even if they are heading in a similar direction.

An understanding of US housing has to link with the politics of race. Since the abolition of slavery, African-Americans have had to fight for their rights in every aspect of their lives, housing included. There is an appalling history of discrimination and racism preventing black people from living in particular places through formal or informal segregation, violence or economic bias that favoured whites. The heroic struggles of the civil rights movement secured important legal reforms, and the symbolism of electing a non-white President in 2008 demonstrates that most Americans are not as bigoted as a minority still are. Nonetheless, as with every other indicator of social inequality, the worst housing conditions are disproportionately likely to be experienced by African-Americans and other non-white ethnic groups.

As Mel King argues, this history of bigotry and injustice gives housing campaigns in the US an existential quality, where demands for better living conditions are couched in terms of basic, universal human rights. This connection is expressed in Boston by Miloon Kothari, the former United Nations Special Rapporteur on the Right to Affordable Housing, now a professor at Massachusetts Institute of Technology (MIT), who says:

> The possibilities of the Right to the City movement are enormous. The concept can be a very powerful organising principle around which the rights of vulnerable populations in cities can be realized. The essential idea is that everyone who lives in the city has a right to what the city has to offer. The limitations occur when the collective concept runs against the vision of policy makers who view the city as a terrain for the accumulation of wealth – not a space where everyone can enjoy what cities have to offer.[43]

In September 2013, Raquel Rolnik, Miloon Kothari's successor at the UN, visited the UK and caused the Coalition government serious discomfort by criticising its housing policies as contrary to the right to adequate housing enshrined in UN statutes.[44]

Framing housing demands in terms of rights has growing relevance in the UK, but it is more embedded in US campaigns, reflecting other political and cultural differences. At a basic level, there is a brutality in American policy that's generally beyond the UK experience. In October 2014, Boston city authorities closed a bridge linking an island in Quincy Bay to the mainland, citing structural defects. This entailed the closure of a homeless hostel on the island which provided services to 700 people a night, many of them recovering from addiction problems. They were all removed under police guard and taken to temporary shelters.[45] In March 2015, the bridge

---

[43] Interview with rabble.ca blog, 7th July 2012.
[44] "Bedroom tax victims 'going hungry and pushed to brink of suicide'", *Daily Mirror*, 12th September 2013.
[45] "Year since Long Island's close finds safety net tattered", *Boston Globe*, 8th October 2015.

was blown up, thus preventing any attempt to return, although engineers had previously stated there was no technical reason to close the bridge. Some commentary in the local media focused on the impact of the shelters on other residents and their property prices, with little apparent sympathy for those displaced. There was also speculation about alternative uses for the island, noting its picturesque location, particularly with the (subsequently abandoned) Olympic bid in the offing. Meanwhile, hundreds of homeless people, severed from their network of support, were scattered throughout the city and soon encountered life-threatening weather conditions. During one of the coldest winters on record, shelters reported a significant increase in the estimated 17,000 Bostonians registered as homeless.

Egleston Square, JP

An example of the energy and complexity that infuses US housing campaigns is found at Egleston Square in the Jamaica Plain (JP) area of Boston. It's also a case that resonates with experiences in the UK. In April 2015, a proposal to build new apartments at 3200 Washington Street, in the Egleston Square neighbourhood, sparked an almost spontaneous outcry, particularly from local young people demanding 100 per cent affordable housing for the site. A coalition of community organisations, including Bikes not Bombs, Reclaim Boston and local churches, met for a "cook out" and then marched through the area with placards reading "Stop Gentrifying Egleston". Alongside the much bigger changes that have taken place throughout the city, this reaction to a plan to build a relatively small number of homes (76), with the usual modest proportion (24 per cent) of so-called affordable units, surprised the development team and politicians. It produced an unsympathetic on-line response from some Bostonians who suggested the local community should be grateful for what they were getting.

Planning approval for the project was deadlocked at the Jamaica Plain Neighbourhood Council Zoning Committee in June 2015, with concerns expressed that a poor precedent would be set for wholesale transformation of the surrounding area. Predictably, the local business community strongly backed redevelopment and the potential boost to commercial activity in a neighbourhood depicted by the authorities as in need of "place making", although as one campaigner said "Egleston Square is already a place". Also in the wings was a non-profit organisation keen to promote a purportedly more sensitive approach to urban regeneration.

In July 2015, the original scheme was comprehensively rejected at another level of municipal decision making (the Jamaica Plain Neighbourhood Council) and approval was deferred again at a subsequent appeal. Despite this, two more public agencies, the Boston Redevelopment Agency (BRA) and the Department of Neighbourhood Development (DND), proceeded with appointing contractors for an adjoining "problem property" (52 Montebello Road) where it was hoped additional affordable housing would be located. The city authorities also launched a "new vision" for a comprehensive "transit-oriented" plan for what they now referred to as the Washington Street Corridor.

The dark arts of urban planning

The Egleston Square case contains the key elements (and a lot of the jargon!) of current urban policy on both sides of the Atlantic. The labyrinthine US planning or "zoning" process bears a legal and cultural similarity to the UK system. Since the principles of planned urban development were codified and professionalised in the early 20th century, US and UK theorists have tried to understand its shifting meanings. These fluctuations revolve around the extent to which local communities can be involved in and influence decisions about what gets built where, by whom and for who. The planning discipline has passed through phases in which it assumed an authoritarian rigidity at one extreme and embraced a collaborative, participative approach at the other. It has now arrived at an uncomfortable hybrid in which planners seek (and legally require) resident involvement, but are often criticised for using this consultation as cover to rubber stamp decisions. The complexity of the planning system disadvantages the ability of people and campaigns to challenge the relentless property development machine. If anything, this power imbalance is even greater in America, which has a peculiarly bureaucratic form of government capable of intimidating and grinding down opposition even more effectively than its British counterpart. These issues are magnified at Egleston Square where the weight of city political and financial power is deployed in support of what are presented as the inherent benefits of regeneration.

In Jamaica Plain, as in most other places, residents have expressed concern about high-rise blocks and the impact of swelling local populations. But there are also fears that new development will jeopardise local identity and that the character of the area will be changed in a way that excludes existing residents. The proposals for Egleston Square make great play on the "mix" it's claimed will revitalise the area, but these assertions encounter deep scepticism that people on low or average incomes will be able to afford the new homes.

Define affordability

The problem of affordability has become the most vexed of contemporary housing policy in the US and UK, at least from the point of view of tenants and others in housing need. The issue causes mounting frustration as different parties wrestle with slippery definitions. At root is a fundamental question about people's ability to meet the cost of a basic human need. Various formulae have been used to try to assess the proportion of a household's income that can be spent on housing and be deemed affordable, the most widely recognised being 30 per cent. However, this neat equation has vanishing relevance against the background of escalating rents and house prices alongside falling or stagnating incomes and a diminishing supply of public, council or other non-market housing. In the 1950s, Americans and Britons typically spent 10 per cent or less of their income on rent. Today an increasing number spend 50 per cent or more.

Arriving at a realistic assessment of what is affordable housing is made even more difficult by the deliberate manipulation of the term by property developers, policy makers and politicians. It is now common in the US and UK for housing marketed at people earning well above Area Median Incomes (AMI) to be described as affordable. This allows developers to obtain planning permission to build and politicians to claim to be meeting targets for affordable homes, but without addressing housing need for those with low and medium incomes. In many places, in both the US and UK, campaigners now argue the real definition of "affordable" housing is that it's unaffordable.

This conflict heightens tensions around places like Egleston Square, where Zoning Committee member Bernie Doherty, addressing developers on 20th June 2015, asked: "I lived here until I was 20. It was good for working people then. Define affordability. What are your rents?" He was told that 75 per cent of the new apartments would be at market rents of $1,400 for a studio, $1,600 for a one bedroom, $1,900 for a two and $2,400 for a three bedroom apartment. Doherty replied "This is not affordable. You can't say these are affordable rents for working people. This is before they pay utilities and everything else. Bring those rents down."

However, the developers successfully defended the project because it complied with targets for affordable housing set by the Mayor of Boston. But these policies relate to an AMI of $70,000 when the average income of private renters in the city is $37,000 and many Jamaica Plain residents have considerably less. A more realistic measurement of affordability is provided by the National Low Income Housing Coalition (NLIHC), who calculate that to afford a monthly rent of $1,300 in the Boston area requires what NLIHC calls a "housing wage" of $25 an hour. For people earning the minimum wage of $8 per hour, that would require a working week of 125 hours!

After numerous meetings and having passed through multiple layers of municipal decision-making, the Washington Street/Montebello Road development at Egleston Square was finally given approval in half an hour on 13th August 2015. Predictably, the Boston Redevelopment Agency voted 4-1 in favour of the scheme, citing its compliance with existing policy, including affordable housing targets. No members of the public were permitted to speak. Outside a demonstration continued to chant for homes that could be afforded by those on low incomes, but it fell on deaf ears.[46]

The Culture of Contentment

Such is the overwhelming experience of housing and community campaigners in the US and UK. The ever-increasing numbers of homeless, of people on housing waiting lists or in sub-standard and insecure accommodation starkly illustrate the failure of market-driven, property developer-dominated housing policy. Yet this has been the norm on both sides of the Atlantic for decades. No single factor adequately explains this chronic disjunction between popular concerns and public policy. However, in one of his last works, the economist J K Galbraith describes the failure of democracy reflected in the inability of the State to respond to the needs of the discontented in the face of the overwhelming political domination of the contented.[47] In an echo of Michael Kane's conversation with the HUD officer, Galbraith attributes this divide to the fact that, in general, people are less likely to vote the less well-off they are. This democratic deficit is enlarged in relation to housing because, in both the US and UK, notions of citizenship and entitlement are increasingly bound up with tenure. Despite the growing numbers who do so, renters in general and public sector tenants in particular are often portrayed as those who have failed to achieve the desired social norm of home ownership and are therefore less deserving of political representation.

---

[46] In May 2016, the Zoning Committee was found to have breached its own rules when granting permission for the project, causing further delays and in October 2016 the Washington Street site was sold by the original developers, casting more uncertainty about the final scheme.

[47] Galbraith J K (1993) *The Culture of Contentment*, Boston, Houghton Mifflin.

This inequality is compounded by policies that undermine stability in the rented sector. Transience has always been a feature of private renting, but increases with the erosion of tenants' rights alongside a rapacious housing market. Constant moves weaken the ability of tenants to organise and insecurity of tenure can intimidate them from attempting to do so. These malign forces are spreading. The future of UK council housing is being undermined by uncertainty, particularly since the Housing and Planning Act, which is also exposing housing association tenants to aggressive commercial practices by their landlords. The scarcity of non-market housing alternatives and the introduction of new types of tenancy that are time limited, means tested and in some cases, conditional on certain types of behaviour are all contributing to the erosion of the social fabric of working class communities. In both the US and UK the clock is turning back to an earlier housing age of marginal existence at the whim of private landlordism.

Conclusion

The short history of the United States of America can be read as a struggle for land and property. Much of that history began in Boston, where the struggle continues. Despite disappointment in establishment quarters at the failed Olympic bid, Boston continues to promote itself as a "boom" city and this is reflected in its overheated, unbalanced housing market. When describing the *Culture of Contentment*, J K Galbraith refers explicitly to the economic unsustainability of State-sponsored property speculation. He also warns of the ruinous social consequences of a society increasingly divided between those favoured with government spending and those consigned to a status of lesser-citizenship. As Mel King argues, such inequality raises questions not just of housing policy, but of fundamental human rights and dignity. These issues are being played out in housing struggles across America, but are magnified on an almost inconceivable scale in the quintessential American city, New York.

2

New York City: You've got money on your mind

Introduction

The 13 mile long, two mile wide spit of land purchased by the Dutch West India Company from the Lenape Indians for 60 guilders in 1626 has come to symbolise the excesses of global speculative property development. But the Manhattan skyscrapers are no more representative of New York City (NYC) than the Eiffel Tower is of Paris. For millions, life is a relentless battle to maintain a foothold in a city where the cost of living is effectively the cost of housing. Like other places with a cavernous income gap, the NYC housing market is horribly distorted. On one side are multi-million dollar apartments consuming a disproportionate amount of space, wealth and political privilege. On the other are long-established working class communities threatened by the dismantling of a system of rent control and public and other non-market housing, which for generations has nurtured the ethnic and cultural diversity that gives the city its special character. But, as in Boston, campaigners are resisting colonialist forces once again attempting to displace them.

It ain't necessarily so

There are several places near Manhattan that offer an alternative to its brutal, commercial gigantism. They defy stereotypes of American individualism and provide more evidence of US/UK housing links. A 45-minute train ride from Penn Street station is Radburn, New Jersey a town that captures some of the contradictory forces that define 20th century American housing and habits. The township of 600 homes, set amongst peaceful woodlands and landscaped open spaces, is a monument to Ebenezer Howard, the visionary from London who in 1902 established the principles of the Garden City.[48] Howard, like Sidney Waterlow and other early 20th century reformers, wanted to find a solution to the congestion and squalor of the industrial city. He'd witnessed these conditions in the 1870s while living in Chicago, a period when the city's popu-

---

[48] Howard E (1902) *Garden Cities of Tomorrow*, London, Faber and Faber (1965 edition).

lation exploded from 12,000 to 307,000. But during his American sojourn, Howard also spent time as a frontier farmer. An attempt to synthesise the benefits of town and country underpinned his vision of building places where people could live in a healthy environment with low rents, high wages and a spirit of freedom and cooperation. During his lifetime, Howard only saw his theories put into practice in two places: Letchworth and Welwyn Garden City in Hertfordshire, 30 miles north of London, but there have been many imitations since. Like any meta-philosophy, Howard's has been subject to numerous interpretations more or less faithful to his original intentions. But the physical, if not the social, form of his ideals can be found in Radburn.

Radburn was founded in 1929 as a "town for the motor age". This is reflected in the street layout which seeks to separate vehicles from pedestrians and control the flow of cars through residential and recreational areas, particularly by using cul-de-sacs and a network of car-free footpaths. The Radburn Model has been widely imitated elsewhere, including large inter-war UK council estates and post-war New Towns. But perhaps more than physical qualities, what distinguishes Radburn is the aim of creating a suburban arcadia with communitarian ideals. Homes are deliberately clustered to encourage social exchanges and avoid the regimental anonymity associated with more typical suburbs. Radburn also eschews the uniform rectilinear and grid layout of most American towns and cities, a system that developed explicitly to facilitate the buying and selling of land.[49] The chief planner of Radburn, Clarence Stein, received his architectural education in Europe, exchanged experiences with UK Garden City advocates and explored ideas of co-operative ownership of workers' housing. Like Howard, he hoped Radburn would provide a template for a network of planned, economically self-sustaining communities

---

[49] Linklater A (2002) *Measuring America: How the United States was shaped by the greatest land sale in history*, London, HarperCollins.

Radburn, New Jersey.

where, rather than being dictated by the individualism of the property market, residents would transcend privatised domesticity through a wider set of shared values. Like Howard, Stein was disappointed. Radburn didn't achieve the social diversity he hoped for and in the wake of the Great Depression, was never able to develop beyond its original narrow footprint. It has, in essence, become an exclusive private housing development, albeit one with an unusual history and character.

It is possible to dismiss Radburn and its older UK cousins, Letchworth and Welwyn Garden City, as anachronistic exceptions, but they do demonstrate the potential for building places freed from the tyranny of commercial domination. More counter-intuitive American housing in the NYC area can be found opposite Van Cortlandt Park in the Bronx, where, in 1927, the Amalgamated Clothing Workers Union (ACW) built the first 300 of what is today a beau-

The Amalgamated Housing Co-op.

tiful 1,500-home development of non-profit, cooperative homes, the oldest of its kind in the US. The Amalgamated was inspired by the determination of Abraham Kazan, a passionate advocate of co-operativism, and Sidney Hillman, a union activist and former member of the revolutionary Bund movement in his native Russia. Together they wanted to build decent homes for ACW members and other working class people living in New York's overcrowded slums.[50] Kazan continued to champion co-operative principles, taking advantage of legislation encouraging non-market housing, such as the 1955 New York state-wide Mitchell-Lama programme that provided low-cost public finance for affordable housing and led to the building of 100,000 homes for people on moderate incomes, 10,000 of them in NYC.

One of the places that resulted from this enlightened wave of housing policy was the 6,000-home Rochdale Village[51] development in Queens, built in 1965 and named in honour of the UK town where the co-operative movement was born. Clarence Stein was an advisor to the project and the Radburn influence is clear. There are local schools, a library, community facilities, abundant landscaped gardens, allotments and a shopping precinct reminiscent of the type found in UK New Towns of the same period. The founding rules of co-operative housing, some inherited directly from the Lancashire pioneers, are still displayed on notice boards around Rochdale Village, including "Open membership with no restriction as to race, creed or colour", "Limited interest on invested share capital", "Political and religious neutrality" and "Continuing education".

The most important feature of Rochdale Village is that it is effectively removed from the speculative property market. Like other Mitchell-Lama and limited equity housing developments, residents are prevented from full, individual ownership of their home and

---

[50] For a flavour of housing in early 20th century New York City, the Tenement Museum in Orchard Street is highly recommended.

[51] Eisenstadt P (2010) *Rochdale Village: Robert Moses, 6,000 Families and New York City's Experiment in Integrated Housing*, Ithaca, Cornell University Press.

Rochdale Village.

therefore from selling for personal profit. In the aftermath of the subprime crash, hundreds of working class families in the surrounding streets of Queens lost their homes due to foreclosure. Nobody at Rochdale Village did, just as no UK council tenant has been made homeless because of "market failure".

NYCHA

Mitchell-Lama and co-operatives built by trade unions are only two examples of numerous types of non-market housing in NYC, but by far the biggest is public housing. With typical chutzpah, the city claimed the original public housing in the US by naming it First Houses,[52] 122 apartments built in 1935 on East 3rd Street, using similar powers that enabled the London County Council to build

---

[52] There are competing claims for the now demolished Techwood Homes in Atlanta, built around the same time.

the Boundary Estate 35 years earlier. At the opening ceremony, one of President Roosevelt's New Deal advisors, Harry Hopkins, made an observation that echoes down the years: "Private capital has never spent a dime to build a house for a poor person."

First Houses has stood the test of time. Its secluded courtyard is still enjoyed by tenants like 94 year-old Mary Hladek, a resident since 1944, and her son Jim, who credits public housing with providing a settled, secure environment to grow up in and "making me the person I am". Today the New York City Housing Authority (NYCHA) owns and manages 178,000 homes, 15 per cent of the national total, almost all of them in high-rise blocks lived in by at least 400,000 New Yorkers. Nicholas Dagen Bloom describes this "valuable reservoir of affordable housing in a pricey global city" as evidence of "public housing that worked".[53] The reasons for NYCHA's success, compared with public housing authorities (PHAs) elsewhere, are complex but defy negative stereotypes in several ways. New York is not demolishing its high rises, unlike other cities making a lazy association between multi-storey blocks and "failed" public housing. Likewise, despite the scale of the task, NYCHA has maintained buildings and services while other PHAs have run theirs down. This contrast was graphically illustrated in the aftermath of hurricane Sandy in 2012: NYCHA recovered from storm damage, whereas the New Orleans PHA used hurricane Katrina in 2005 as a pretext for demolition. The context of New York public housing in a city with a diverse economy and population has challenged other prejudicial associations. Only 12 per cent of NYCHA tenants are on welfare, 47 per cent are working families. NYCHA tenants pay an average rent of $483 per month, capped at 30 per cent of income. Despite a system of rent regulation, average New York rents in the private sector are $2,700 a month, 58 per cent of median income. Unsurprisingly, NYCHA tenants stay put

---

[53] Dagen Bloom N (2008) *Public Housing that Worked: New York in the Twentieth Century*, Philadelphia, University of Pennsylvania Press.

Mary Hladek and her son Jim, First Houses.

for an average of 22 years (there's no right to buy in US public housing) and there are 258,800 people on the waiting list.[54] Nonetheless, what NYCHA has in common with all public housing is an acute financial crisis on a scale beyond that of other PHAs, with a budget deficit of $77 million and a repairs backlog of $18 billion.

Rent control

Alongside public housing, rent control is perhaps the thing that most challenges the image of New York as the capital of free market excess. Controls protect two million private sector tenants, a protection not yet won by UK private renters. Providing an antidote to rampant private landlordism resulted from long grass-roots campaigns

---

[54] Figures from NYCHA (2016) *Facts about NYCHA*.

driving legislative reform. Today's super-exploitation and hyper-gap between rich and poor in NYC is nothing new. At the end of the 19th century, a typical floor in a five storey tenement on the Lower East Side would be subdivided into four usually overcrowded apartments, each paying around $10 a month rent. A Manhattan block was thus able to generate an income of $12,000 a month for a speculative landlord , at a time when the average family lived on $350 a year. The upsurge of union organisation and radicalism, particularly among the immigrant Jewish community of which Abraham Kazan and many of his associates were a product, demanded better conditions at work and at home. As well as taking direct action to build non-market homes, union, communist, socialist, anarchist and liberal activists built campaigns, rent strikes and demonstrations that reached new intensity in the Great Depression. This movement drew attention to the slumlords, but also to the limitations of philanthropy. It demanded rent control alongside public housing. Citywide tenant organisations, augmented by supportive elected politicians, finally achieved what have become lasting rent restrictions in 1943, and as Ronald Lawson observes, established themselves as "a permanent force in the political life of the city".[55] Preserving rent control has become a vital, totemic issue in NYC. As the chair of the city's planning commission, Carl Weisbrod, puts it, rent regulation "is essential for the future of the city, for its economic goals, for social equality, to make a city attractive and available for all, rich, poor and middle class."[56]

After some intense political wrangling, lobbying and campaigning in 2015, New York's system of rent control is safe until 2019.

The power of the burbs

The history and current concerns of housing in NYC has to be set alongside the presence of sprawling suburbia. The idea of living

---

[55] Lawson R (1986) *The Tenant Movement in New York City 1904 – 1984.*
[56] "New York's rent controls: essential for the future of the city", *The Guardian*, 19th August 2015.

outside but within easy reach of the city is as old as antiquity, but has assumed massive physical and ideological significance in the US and to a lesser degree the UK. In 1869 Frederick Law Olmsted and his English colleague Calvert Vaux, who worked together on New York's Central Park, designed a prototype planned suburb – Riverside – nine miles outside Chicago. Inspired by the same impulses that would later motivate Ebenezer Howard (who was in Chicago around that time), Riverside contrasted urban chaos with the order and calm of the countryside. It spawned many imitations, notably Bedford Park in west London, developed between 1875 and 1886 as the first garden suburb in the UK. Howard's garden cities manifesto and its off-spring at Radburn are essentially derivatives of earlier suburban places that offered an escape from the city, but with broader social objectives. Subsequent developments, particularly State-sponsored overspill suburbs and New Towns like Becontree, Stevenage and Milton Keynes in the UK and the truncated New Deal-era greenbelt communities in the US, all attempted to reach beyond narrow goals of building homes. But elsewhere, suburbia has become synonymous with social conservatism. John Betjeman's lyrical celebration of *Metroland* captures the cultural significance of UK suburbs; these are dwarfed, in every sense, by their US equivalents. In his classic book on the subject, Kenneth Jackson said of the American suburbs:

> ...suburbia has become the quintessential physical achievement of the United States; it is perhaps more representative of its culture than big cars, tall buildings, or professional football. Suburbia symbolises the fullest, most unadulterated embodiment of contemporary culture; it is a manifestation of such fundamental characteristics of American society as conspicuous consumption, a reliance upon the private automobile, upward mobility, the separation of the family into nuclear units, the widening division between work and leisure, and a tendency toward racial and economic exclusiveness.[57]

---

[57] Jackson K T (1985) *Crabgrass Frontier: The suburbanisation of the United States* (p4), Oxford, Oxford University Press.

To this litany should be added that suburbia is a manifestation of the recurrent, deep-rooted utopian impulse in American thought and deeds. From the moment Europeans set foot on the continent, the idea that it could be shaped as an ideal society has dominated housing patterns and political ideology. Even after capitalist norms of private profit and property confounded such aspirations, continual attempts have been made to fulfil their promise. These have ranged from the many communities in the Owenite socialist tradition, such as Harmony, Indiana, to religious settlements such as Salt Lake City, experiments in land tax at Arden, Delaware and attempts by messianic private developers to plan and build the perfect place, such as Columbia, Maryland. A more recent example – and one with particular significance for the re-styling of US public housing – is the planned suburb of Seaside, Florida where the 1998 film *The Truman Show*, a satire on suburban idealism, was made. Contemporary exercises in utopian suburbs also exist in the UK, often under the same conceited label of "place making" as found at Egleston Square in Boston. Greenwich Millennium Village in south-east London (not to be confused with its Manhattan namesake) enlists many of the New Urbanist principles of Seaside, but as in the US, has also been used as part of the justification for building private property on public land and diluting municipal housing.

Levittown

The complexity and scale of the suburbs and their place in US society and housing policy are perfectly illustrated at Levittown, Long Island, just east of New York City. When Abraham Levitt and his sons William and Alfred first visited the place that now bears their name, at the end of World War II, it was mostly potato fields. Five years later, *Time* magazine described the 17,000-home settlement as an "achievement of its cultural moment" to rival Venice! Levitt and Sons used innovative assembly line techniques to fast-track the construction of single family homes built to three basic designs. Each stood on its own small plot of land which the Levitts prescribed could not be fenced in, almost a metaphor for the American Dream in itself. Levittown also demonstrates the endemic bias in government support for different types of housing. The initial rent of $60 a month, with an option to buy after a year for $7,990 (including appliances), deliberately targeted demobbed servicemen who would benefit from substantial State-funded mortgage subsidies, provided they were white. Black people were explicitly excluded from Levittown. William Levitt (a second generation Jewish immigrant) adopted a pragmatic, if unprincipled, approach, saying that he could try to solve a housing problem or a race problem but not both. An important civil rights landmark was achieved in 1957 when a black couple, William and Daisy Myers, bought a home at a replica Levittown in Pennsylvania and resisted racist attempts to enforce residential segregation.[58]

Levittown marks a water-shed and an enduring divergence in comparative US/UK housing policy. Between 1945 and 1950 the British government oversaw the building of one million homes, the majority of them owned and let by local authorities, setting a trend that continued for three decades. By contrast, between 1940 and 1960, owner occupation in the US grew from 44 to 62 per cent and throughout that period was 10 per cent higher than in the UK.

Levittown vividly demonstrates that suburbia is as much an ideological construct as a physical one. At the height of the Cold War, William Levitt gave an explicit political justification for promoting home ownership. He said "No one who owns his own house and lot can be a Communist. He has too much to do", an ironic echo of Friedrich Engels' 1872 description of a mortgage as a mechanism of social control. Senator Joseph McCarthy also aligned the suburbs with Americanism and counter-posed their reputed wholesome

---

[58] Kushner D (2009) *Levittown: Two families, one tycoon and the fight for civil rights in America's legendary suburb*, New York, Walker and Company.

Levittown.

values with public housing, which he described as "breeding grounds for communism".

Suburbia, in all its facets, continues to exert a gravitational pull over trans-Atlantic housing policy, but it's important to avoid simplistic explanations of this. As well as predicting the displacement of central Boston's working class community, Herbert Gans provides a balanced account of suburban lifestyles in Levittown that still resonates. Gans acknowledges the problems of social and physical isolation, poor public transport and racism, but suggests something elemental in the quality of life for those admitted to the suburban nirvana:

> The community may displease the professional city planner and intellectual defender of cosmopolitan culture, but perhaps more than any other type of community, Levittown permits most of its residents to

be what they want to be – to centre their lives around the home and the family, to be among neighbours whom they can trust, to find friends to share leisure hours, and to participate in organisations that provide sociability and the opportunity to be of service to others.[59]

However, the nature of the suburbs is changing. Places that for 100 years represented aspiration are increasingly a destination of necessity, not choice. The cost of housing in American and British inner-cities is exerting centrifugal force on those unable to find and keep a home they can afford.

A New York housing story

Cherry Street is in Manhattan's Lower East Side, straddled by the East River and lots of public housing. The tradition of multi-culturalism and working class struggle infuse the area. The Jewish community has largely moved on, but its memory is preserved in many ways, including the naming of NYCHA blocks like Vladeck Houses in honour of inter-war socialist politician and one of the housing authority's first board members Baruch Charney Vladeck. The Lower East Side used to symbolise the worst excesses of private landlordism. Today the area is in the path of the speculative property leviathan stampeding around Manhattan. Building is underway at 227 Cherry Street of a development that captures the social toxicity, narcissism and mania of contemporary housing and urban policy.

The Extell Development Company, whose CEO is the son of a Lower East Side rabbi and whose company name derives from an immodest combination of "excellence" and "intelligence", already has a dozen gargantuan buildings in Manhattan. Their portfolio includes One57, a 75-storey residential block looking down (very literally) on Central Park; the penthouse apartment sold for $100 million, hence its sobriquet "The Billionaire Building". At Cherry Street, Extell bought a riverside site for $175 million, demolished a

---

[59] Gans H J (1967) *The Levittowners* (p64), New York, Pantheon.

Placard from
Cherry Street
demonstration.

neighbourhood supermarket and has started building what it hopes will become a "mixed use", 72-storey tower of 787 luxury private apartments that will block out the sun for the neighbouring public housing residents, many of them from New York's long-established Chinese community.

The project is due for completion in 2019 and is being built on a site identified as a flood hazard area by the government agency heavily criticised for its negligence in New Orleans after Hurricane Katrina. Precise details of the scheme await final approval, but it is a practice of developers to establish facts on the ground by starting construction and using the final composition as bargaining chips with politicians, planning authorities and local communities. What appears certain is there will be no non-market housing at what Extell is branding One Manhattan Square[60], a name with no relationship to existing local geography. Instead, there will be a separate 13-storey block of 205 homes for people on moderate incomes. These homes will be allocated by lottery! Separate entrances, or "poor doors", for different types of residents have become commonplace in new property developments on both sides of the Atlantic, but 227 Cherry Street will amplify the social and physical segregation of the 21st century city. Some of those who buy luxury apartments at 227 Cherry Street are likely to be Chinese. A perverse sign of the iniquitous global trade in housing as a commodity is that overseas investors spending $500,000 or more in the US property market can also acquire access to American citizenship.[61] So, a few Chinese people will obtain a Green Card while intensifying the threat of displacement to many others.

On 27th May 2015, I joined about 100 protesters gathered in Cherry Street with placards (many of them in Chinese characters, some in Spanish, several targeting NYC Mayor Bill de Blasio) familiar to struggles in other places.

---

[60] From October 2016, apartments at One Manhattan Square were being marketed with a starting price of $1,179,000.

[61] "Want a Green Card? Invest in real estate", *New York Times*, 15th May 2015.

No to racism, no to displacement

De Blasio: Protect the Lower East Side, not BIG developers

*72 storey luxury tower, 13 story 'affordable' tower –
what's fair about that?*

De Blasio lies to our community

We need more low income housing, not second-class poor doors

Wherever they arise, the catalyst of such struggles are frequently distilled in one word – gentrification. It's a term that has evolved significantly since it was coined by Ruth Glass in the mid-1960s to describe a practice of middle class people buying and renovating dilapidated homes in Islington, north London. Neil Smith gave the theory of gentrification a distinctive New York exposition in the mid-1990s, focusing on curtailed access to public space and the economic forces leading to the "revanchist" reoccupation of working class neighbourhoods by the affluent.[62] In the mid-2000s, Mike Davidson and Loretta Lees examined the significance of "new build" gentrification, particularly on riverside sites and with State support.[63] These academic theories and many others add something to an understanding of gentrification. But none capture its visceral meaning for working class communities. This threat is stark in Manhattan, where in mid-2015 the average price for an apartment was $1.87 million, the median price was $980,000 and 13,000 more private apartments were due to be built before the end of 2016, in a city where there are an estimated 60,000 homeless people.

---

[62] Smith N (1996) *The New Urban Frontier: Gentrification and the Revanchist City*, London, Routledge.
[63] Davidson M and Lees L (2005) *New-build 'gentrification' and London's riverside renaissance* in Environment and Planning, Vol. 37 pp 1165 – 1190.

Protest at
Cherry
Street.

The global ties that bind us

The cosmopolitan make-up of the Cherry Street anti-Extell demonstration is mirrored by the increasingly global character of the development industry. Numerous links exist between US and UK property interests. For example, the Australian Lendlease company not only built One57 for Extell in Manhattan but is also the lead developer of the former Heygate council estate in south London, one of the most controversial estate redevelopments in the UK. As part of the same project to redevelop the Elephant and Castle area, the self-declared "progressive" developer Essential Living (one of whose directors is a former head of a housing charity) is building a 44-storey block of flats for private rent on public land gifted to them by the former Mayor of London Boris Johnson (also a native New Yorker!). One of Essential Living's goals is to "redefine" private renting, the rapid growth of which is one of the critical points of convergence in US and UK housing. Essential Living are backed to the tune of $200 million by M3 Capital Partners, a US based firm with $3.4 billion of international "real estate investments" and offices in Chicago, New York, London, Hong Kong and Sao Paulo. Among M3's key "products" are Real Estate Investment Trusts (REITs), a model for tax exempt, transnational institutional property speculation with a long history in the US and a growing presence in the UK. Among those flirting with REITS in Britain are some housing associations, so-called "social" landlords now known by the more accurate name Private Registered Providers. In the aftermath of the 2007-08 crash, banks are far more reluctant to lend money for housing. Risky financial products like globally traded REITs are taking their place.

The biggest player in this property market casino is the Blackstone Group, whose CEO raked in $690 million in 2014 (a 50 per cent increase on the previous year). Blackstone is a hydra's head conglomerate that owns the Hilton Hotel group and the Waldorf Astoria in Manhattan as well as retail and commercial property worldwide. They also have a financial stake in many peoples' homes.

In 2013, Blackstone spent $100 million a week in the housing market (although this has slowed significantly since). Scavenging amidst the credit crunch wreckage, Blackstone hoovered up thousands of foreclosed/repossessed family homes around the world. Many of these homes have been repackaged for the booming US rental market in which Blackstone's Invitation Homes subsidiary has 48,000 properties offering a "high quality rental experience", much like the one Essential Living hopes to sell in London. In September 2014, Blackstone stated their intention to invest in UK housing, targeting reincarnated subprime mortgages and Buy-to-Let. In March 2015 Blackstone announced its investment in a US company, Buy to Rent (B2R), with the following intent:

> The transaction is expected to consist of $230,000,000...backed by 144 mortgage loans secured by single-family residential properties, two to four unit properties, condominium properties, townhomes, multifamily properties and mixed-use properties. B2R was established by funds managed by Blackstone Tactical Opportunities to provide residential buy-to-rent mortgages for property investors, focused exclusively on the financing and growth capital needs of single-family home investors and entrepreneurs.[64]

Blackstone is not alone. In the US, eight institutional investor landlords have portfolios of 150,000 homes or more, an important contrast with the private rented sector in the UK which, for the moment at least, is still dominated by small, individual landlords. Among the new breed of acquisitive corporate landlords is Westbrook Partners, a private equity firm based in New York, but with a variety of property interests in cities around the world including London.

In winter 2014, tenants from the New Era estate in Hoxton, east London were faced with the threat of huge rent rises by their new landlord, Westbrook Partners. The high-profile battle, which ended

---

[64] Extracts from Blackstone press release, 27th March 2015.

in a qualified victory for the tenants, highlighted how the UK housing landscape is being re-shaped by US influences and global flows of capital. Westbrook took over New Era from another private landlord which for many years had charged stabilised "fair" rents. Examples of more benign ownership and tenancies in the private rented sector pre-date the watershed of January 1989 and the introduction of Assured Shorthold Tenancies, which decisively shifted the legal balance of power towards private landlords. This paved the way for more speculative investment in the UK private rented sector, demonstrated by the growth of the Buy to Let market. With home ownership increasingly unaffordable and a scarcity of council and other non-market housing, UK private renting has doubled over the last decade and, as in NYC, renters in London and other cities see rent consuming an ever-greater proportion of their income.

Seb Klier, from the UK's Generation Rent campaign, says:

> After almost thirty years of deregulation, the UK's private rented sector has become a disaster for a growing number of tenants. They're now two and a half times more likely to be evicted under the "no fault"[65] procedure than in 2009. Rents – already costing tenants 60 per cent of their incomes in many areas – are projected to rise by 5 per cent annually over the coming years in the most expensive parts of the country. This lack of security and affordability disproportionately affects working class tenants who are increasingly living in the private rented sector and are often forced into the third of privately rented homes that are in poor or unsafe condition.

Committee Against Anti-Asian Violence (CAAAV)

CAAAV was amongst the groups protesting at 227 Cherry Street. As their name suggests, the organisation's origins lie in resisting a

---

[65] Assured Shorthold Tenancies enable landlords to go to court and obtain an automatic eviction order without needing to give a reason.

more physical threat to pan-Asian-American communities, but that assault now comes in different forms. Today CAAAV are particularly concerned with the growing links between the criminal justice system and access to housing. One of their workers, Naved Husain, specifically relates the threat of displacement to the punitive application of tenancy conditions:

> There are lots of rules and regulations in public housing. NYCHA works with the police who use surveillance methods that help kick people out for minor infractions. So a teenager gets caught stealing a candy bar and gets evicted and permanently excluded from NYCHA. This collusion between NYCHA and the police benefits private developers who have plans to buy the projects. These issues particularly affect the black and Latino community.

Naved's comments illustrate another important cultural difference between US and UK housing, particularly in the public sector. In the city of "zero tolerance", housing management norms reflect the underlying sense that living in public housing is not a right but a privilege that can be abruptly withdrawn, even for trivial transgressions. This is reinforced by the close operational relationship between many PHAs and the police.[66] Between 2007 and 2014, 4,698 individuals were permanently excluded by NYCHA. If they were the children of NYCHA tenants, their parents were also at risk of eviction if they allowed their off-spring into their homes. Such stipulations can be enforced by the regular, sometimes unannounced, apartment inspections that are a feature of US public housing.

While UK council landlords have access to similar powers, historically they have tended not to use them. Council housing has come to be regarded as "a home for life". While this view is sometimes exaggerated, the legal protection of a Secure Tenancy, won by

---

[66] During my internship with a PHA in 1992, I spent a lot of time with the housing authority's directly-employed police force.

council tenants in 1980, has been one of the most valued qualities of living in council housing – but it's changing. In the 2011 Localism Act, the UK government signalled the intention to make tenancies time-limited and means-tested, an ambition confirmed by the 2016 Housing and Planning Act. An ideological path had been laid for this potentially decisive shift over several years. In 2008, a Labour housing minister (in her first day in the job) questioned the principles behind secure tenancies. In 2010, Prime Minister David Cameron suggested to council tenants "maybe in five or 10 years you will be doing a different job and be better paid and you won't need that home, you will be able to go into the private sector".[67] In the aftermath of the 2011 riots in the UK, some councils attempted to evict tenants whose children had allegedly been involved in the disturbances. Thus a series of deliberate steps have been taken towards the US model of public housing: tenant's homes being treated as conditional, reinterpreted as "emergency" housing and underpinned by a system of reduced entitlement.

Another key campaign issue for CAAAV is resisting the displacement of low-income (and therefore disproportionately black, Latino and Asian) households from the city, squeezed out by NYC's deformed housing market. But the urban exodus is a class phenomenon rather than an ethnic one. The Brookings Institute has found that "the economically turbulent 2000s have redrawn America's map of poverty".[68] During this period, white Americans became more likely to live in poor suburbs, although blacks and Latinos still lived in the suburban areas with the highest concentrations of poverty. A very similar process is unfolding in the UK. The combined effect of insufficient council and non-market rented housing, rent rises and benefit cuts, led to a 28 per cent increase in the number of households being rehoused by local authorities

---

[67] "David Cameron wants fixed-term council house tenancies", *The Independent*, 3rd August 2010.
[68] "The Growth and Spread of Concentrated Poverty, 2000 to 2008 – 2012", Brookings Interactive, 31st July 2014.

outside of London in 2014-15. Throughout the UK there is evidence of people being priced out of cities and there has also been a significant rise in suburban poverty.[69]

For CAAAV campaigners the future of their city is at stake as the result of political decisions that are skewing housing policies towards the well-off, with multiple consequences for others:

> People from Chinatown are moving to the outer Bronx and Flushing, but they're still working here. The further they go, the more affordable the housing, but the longer and more expensive their journey to work. These are strains that make life difficult for people. It's happening all over America. The rich people live in the city with all its amenities and the poor are pushed out. New York City's becoming a playground for the 1%. (Naved Husain, CAAAV)

The CASA vision for the Bronx

New Yorkers aren't passively accepting social and ethnic cleansing. The Community Action for Safer Apartments (CASA) campaign provides another example of the dynamic struggles for housing justice in America. CASA is part of a multi-service community organisation based on the Settlement model that originated in the 1880s at Toynbee Hall in the East End of London and quickly spawned US imitations. CASA is based in what the New York City planning department now refers to as "Cromwell-Jerome", a two-mile stretch of the Bronx where the majority of the population are Latino, 90 per cent rent privately, and where the authorities hope to create "a new neighbourhood". As in Boston and many other places, this exercise in putative urban renaissance is concentrating opposition to an entire model of autocratic urban policy.

Like his Boston counterpart, New York City's Mayor de Blasio has a political imperative to address the housing crisis, which he hopes to do by building or preserving 200,000 affordable homes over the

---

[69] The Smith Institute (2014) *Poverty in Suburbia.*

next decade. Cromwell-Jerome has been identified as one of the places for doing so, subject to a "re-zoning" that would enable more residential uses and make the area, currently heavily inhabited by small businesses including many garages and car repair shops, more attractive. The point of conflict for CASA and other groups working to develop an alternative community vision for the Bronx is the sense that consultation is not genuine and, in particular, that the authorities are hiding the true meaning and impact of the envisaged affordable housing.

Interpreting already contentious definitions of "affordable" is made more difficult and divisive by policies that deliberately salami-slice the provision of new homes according to targeted gradations of income. This process, sometimes referred to as "inclusionary zoning", has been refined to a fine art by many US public authorities. It is assuming more significance in the UK as access to housing becomes increasingly means-tested. New York's housing plan identifies five income bands related to Area Median Income (AMI) and the amount a household can pay without becoming "burdened" by a rent that is over 30 per cent of their income. Mayor de Blasio's stated aim is that the majority of new homes will be affordable to those on "low, very low and extremely low" incomes. But this apparently progressive and equitable strategy has been dismissed as a Trojan horse for gentrification by many campaigners who have seen such promises broken in the past.

The provision of non-market homes has become part of the bargaining process between private developers and public authorities in the US and UK. In practice, the targets have been missed. Between 2005 and 2013, under the previous Mayor Bloomberg, inclusionary zoning contributed only 1.7 per cent of new homes, during a period in which New York City was increasingly socially and economically polarised. Affordable housing policies in the UK have led to similar, though not as bad, failings. During the reputedly enlightened years when Ken Livingstone was Mayor of London (2000 – 2008), less than 20 per cent of new homes were for affordable social rents, from a stated target of 50 per cent.[70] There are signs that the current London Mayor, Sadiq Khan (elected May 2016), is adopting an approach to new affordable housing similar to NYC's Bill de Blasio.

Gross income inequality, the over-heated housing market and statistical sophistry undermine existing affordable housing policies. There are sizeable differences between the AMI for the wider New York City area ($77,000) and the city itself ($50,000). For the Cromwell-Jerome neighbourhood, AMI is $25,000 and ten per cent of the population have income below $15,000. In some cases NYC developers have been allowed to build homes for households with income of $135,000 with rents of $3,380 per month and still call them 'affordable'! This absurdity finds its UK parallel in the form of government-subsidised Starter Homes costing up to £450,000, defined as affordable under the Housing and Planning Act.[71]

CASA and a coalition of other Bronx-based community organisations, including trade unions, see the re-zoning of Cromwell-Jerome as a harbinger of rising land prices, speculative property investment and displacement. Under the slogan "Nothing about us, without us, is for us" they want a planning process that is genuinely participative, protection against eviction by opportunist landlords, decent jobs and for the price of any new homes to reflect the incomes of the existing population.

Life across the Hudson

The New York development frenzy ripples out from Manhattan. In the 1990s, Jersey City was widely perceived as a grim symbol of the dying, de-industrialised American metropolis. Today it's a shimmering reflection of Wall Street on the other side of the Hudson River. Where there were once abandoned wharves and derelict

---

[70] Bowie D (2010) *Politics, Planning and Homes in a World City*, Abingdon, Routledge.
[71] Under pressure, the Conservative government is reviewing this policy.

factories there are now high-rise apartment blocks and hotels. The only comparable social and physical transformation in the UK is London's Docklands. In March 2015, global property consultants CBRE commented "The hottest place for New York City money is in Jersey City". The astonishing pace and scale of change, with accompanying hyperbole, has inevitable consequences for those unable or unwilling to participate in the property jamboree. Around Journal Square, the city's main transport and civic centre, scores of dispossessed people contemplate their futures as another high-rise development reaches for the sky. There's been a 12 per cent increase in local homelessness in the last year. As Jersey City native Devyn Manibo puts it "When Jersey City becomes a commodity, it's no longer a home".[72]

I first visited Jersey City in 1992. When I told the US customs officer at Newark airport where I was going, he said "Why would you want to go there?" I was going to work as an intern for the Jersey City Public Housing Authority (JCHA). It was a seminal experience that fundamentally shaped my understanding of housing and convinced me of the dangers for the UK in pursuing a US-style policy of under-investment, privatisation and stigmatisation in relation to council housing.

Revisiting JCHA 23 years later, I found changes reflecting the city as a whole and the national restructuring of public housing. Previously hard pressed but essentially successful developments of homes for thousands of low income people were now changed beyond recognition or abandoned. The A. Harry Moore development, formerly home to 2,000 people in 656 apartments, is undergoing redesign typical of public housing throughout the US. Financed by HOPE VI and inspired by New Urbanist design, high-rise blocks have been demolished and replaced with approximately 400 mixed income town houses and apartments, with an

---

[72] "Campaign urges locals to take Jersey City back from gentrification", *NJ.com*, 15th June 2015.

additional quota of off-site homes in another part of the city. This means a net loss of rented public housing and segmented alterations to the tenure pattern further restricting access by targeting specific income groups. For example, Phase III of the redevelopment will produce 116 new homes consisting of:

35 JCHA homes for households with income up to 60 per cent of AMI

25 "Project Based Voucher" for households with income up to 50 per cent AMI

34 "Tax Credit" homes for households with income between 45 per cent and 60 per cent AMI

10 JCHA homes defined as "workforce housing" for households with 60 – 80 per cent AMI

12 "market rate homes"

In effect, only 40 per cent of the new homes remain under JCHA management and access to these is conditional on income. The remainder are in the private sector, with access restricted by a combination of income level and voucher entitlement (for which JCHA currently has a waiting list of 1,800). The redevelopment of A. Harry Moore is a microcosm of the national trend. The Tax Credit system is effectively another form of speculative investment by which private developers receive de facto, but hidden, public subsidies to build non-market homes in return for tax breaks. There's growing interest in this system from UK housing associations as they become both more commercially-oriented and attempt to fill the gap left by diminishing direct government investment.[73]

In another part of Jersey City but significantly closer to the "Gold Coast" of the Hudson River is the 451-home Montgomery Gardens site, a place I once knew as vibrant testimony to careful manage-

---

[73] *Funding housing for older people and supported housing: US Low Income Housing Tax Credits and their use in the UK*, Housing Learning and Improvement Network, research paper, December 2014.

ment and the respectful involvement of tenants in the running of their homes. Today it's deserted. Its empty buildings are covered in security shutters. Weeds, instead of children, flourish in its playgrounds. Montgomery Gardens is due to be redeveloped as part of a Choice Neighbourhoods Initiative (CNI),[74] a HUD programme launched in 2010 and similar to the UK's much-vaunted but patchily successful New Deal for Communities (NDC).

Public-Private Partnerships are intrinsic to such policies and at Montgomery Gardens, Manhattan-based real estate investors Metrovest Equities aim to increase their portfolio of "obsolete, institutionally-owned properties". Final details and funding for "transforming" Montgomery Gardens have yet to be confirmed. But experience elsewhere suggests the biggest winners will be those able to make money from the process. CNI is presented as a more palatable version of HOPE VI, pledging that more genuinely affordable homes will be protected and replaced as part of large-scale regeneration programmes. Time will tell. But there's no doubt that CNI continues the overall policy trend of reducing and ultimately eliminating the role of public, non-profit and democratically accountable bodies as direct providers of housing.

Some advocates for affordable homes say that in the context of neoliberal domination, pragmatism demands flexibility in how non-market housing is provided – particularly for the poorest – and by whom. There's an argument that a change of landlord and shifts in tenure patterns are a price worth paying for preserving at least some level of affordable housing. This was what supporters of UK stock transfer maintained. However, such a position risks glossing over and legitimising the divisiveness and commercial motivations implicit in NDC and CNI, the long-term social damage of which outlast any short-term physical improvements.

---

[74] There is now doubt about the future of the Choice Neighbourhood Initiative and other housing programmes, following the announcement of proposed cuts in the HUD budget by the new Trump administration.

Waiting list closed

The first thing you see on the JCHA website, in red text and underlined, is "Public housing waiting list is closed". Meeting one of the organisation's senior managers (on condition of anonymity) affords an insight behind this stark message. She's worked for the organisation for over 20 years, seen its fluctuating fortunes and adopts the pragmatism characteristic of many long-serving housing workers. Ms X is acutely aware of the organisation's responsibility as the biggest single landlord in Jersey City. With echoes of Boston and New York, but on a smaller scale, JCHA has a repairs backlog of $175 million, to be found from an annual budget of $4 million, and is therefore compelled to explore alternative funding. As Ms X puts it "We can't keep putting band-aids on the 1940s buildings". The biggest change Ms X has witnessed has been the 50 per cent reduction in homes directly owned and managed by JCHA, surpassed by a voucher programme now double their permanent accommodation. Ms X is very clear about the overall intention of these changes:

> Federal government is trying to get out of the housing business, but that's going to be hard to do. There are 3,200 PHAs and two million tenants. You can't make them all homeless, but then again, HUD spelt backwards is 'Duh?'

Ms X foresees JCHA being forced to merge with other City departments and adopt an ever-more entrepreneurial approach, but (as a reasonably well-paid public employee) her most telling comment on life across the Hudson is "I was born and raised in Jersey City, but I had to move out. I can't afford it any more".

Conclusions

Distilling the housing essence of New York City is almost impossible. But the hidden truth about the ultimate capitalist city is that it's dependent on non-market housing. It could not be the dynamic, diverse place it is without the combination of public housing, rent

control and various other forms of sub- and non-market accommodation that enable people from a variety of economic backgrounds
to live there. But these are at risk and are already diluting. The
outward migration of low and medium income households poses
a double threat. First, the city becomes more polarised as housing
costs escalate beyond the reach of all but the wealthy, and non-
market and temporary alternatives becomes a residual refuge for
the poor. Second, "moving out" switches from aspiration to compul-
sion, causing social and economic dislocation. The policies of a
reputedly progressive Mayor aim to prevent this scenario. But he
wants to do so by riding the tiger of massive financial interests
which so far shown no sign they share his vision of a "just city".

3

Sweet home Chicago?

Introduction

Despite New York City's omnipresent image, in some respects Chicago is more representative of the American experience. Its history captures the seismic growth of the nation in the 19th century, its emergence as a "super power" in the 20th and its fractured identity in the 21st. During all these periods, Chicago's housing policy has reflected and at times led wider trends. Today the city presents the American housing crisis on a scale that should be of deep concern.

Chicago is noted for its architecture. As well as boasting the first planned suburb at Riverside, the city has inspired a succession of other innovations in building design and technology that have directly influenced the shape of our homes: the first metal-framed tower blocks; the City Beautiful movement showcased at the Columbian Exposition held in Chicago in 1893; the work of Frank Lloyd Wright, who gave a unique expression to the ideal of an American Home. But design is not the most important aspect of housing policy. Simplistic associations have frequently been made between how a building looks and how it functions as a home. Aesthetic considerations, though important, are intrinsically subjective. Sadly, a great deal of damage has been done to the reputation of public housing, in the US and UK, by those who object to it because of how it looks. The prejudice, often promoted by those with a vested interest, against certain architectural styles has too often been allowed to skew, determine and justify housing policy decisions. In Chicago it's been done on a city-wide scale.

The absurd proposition that high-rise blocks "don't work" is contradicted by the willingness of people with money to spend vast amounts to live in them, including some that were once publically owned. Keeling House in Bethnal Green, east London for example, was the first council tower block to be listed for its architectural quality. After structural problems emerged, it was later condemned as a symbol of policy failure. It was then privatised and after significant investment, a two-bedroom flat in Keeling House now costs over £500,000 to buy, over £2,000 a month to rent. This truncated life-cycle illustrates that architectural judgements are often based on class and financial values, rather than policy or technical ones. Some people are willing to pay up to £.3.3 million to live in London's Barbican Centre, the acme of high-rise, concrete, Modernist architecture, or $100 million to live in a tower block above Central Park.

Chicago is also home to one of the earliest and most ambitious experiments in providing comprehensive social services to working class communities and in particular to women. Hull House on South Halsted Street was established by Jane Addams in 1889 following her visit to its London progenitor, Toynbee Hall. Over the next 45 years Addams oversaw the development of nurseries, play areas, leisure and educational facilities, midwifery services, a theatre and other activities occupying an entire block of buildings. Hull House residents and affiliates also supported local labour disputes and took part in campaigns for female suffrage, immigrant rights, safety at work and improved housing conditions. Like many working class neighbourhoods, the area around Hull House fell victim to 1960s "urban renewal" and like many other places, the sponsor and benefactor of this inner-city land-grab was a university. In a further sad irony, the charity that emerged from Hull House and continued to provide social services to under-privileged Chicagoans went bust in 2012.

South Side

There are some places the media finds hard to describe without using the word 'notorious'. Chicago's South Side is one of them. A panoply of associations is conjured by the name: crime, poverty, drugs, gangs, violence and – whether coded or not – black. As ever, such generalisations conceal social and geographic complexity. Like London's East End or Los Angeles' South Central, even defining the area is difficult. The boundaries shift with time and perspective. By one interpretation, South Side's borders are the city's Loop or commercial district at 18th Street to the north, Lake Michigan to the east, 79th Street to the south and a jagged line adjacent to State Street on the west, an area of approximately ten square miles. Other designations draw a bigger or smaller map. Within the South Side catch-all are many distinct neighbourhoods. Barack Obama owns a home and plans to build a Presidential Library there. The South Side contains affluence alongside deprivation and some want to replace one with the other.

Ten years ago, Herman Bonner was threatened with eviction from his home in the Bronzeville area of the South Side, where he was born and has lived most his life. He's been involved in housing campaigns ever since. Herman has seen enormous changes in his neighbourhood, a place suffused with the cultural history of the African-American community that arrived in Chicago during the Great Migration from the southern states in the 1930s and 1940s. Herman was born in 1958, one of the first residents of the Stateway Gardens public housing development, part of the mass housing initiative which produced 22,000 Chicago Housing Authority (CHA) homes between 1950 and 1970. Herman recalls Stateway as a place where "everybody knew you, so you were pretty much safe".

There's been a grim link between CHA and violence, often portrayed with an assumption, rather than proof, of causality. More-over, it is impossible to make any balanced judgment of Chicago's public housing without placing it firmly in the context of a city (and country) deeply ingrained with institutional racism. Like all US public housing, Chicago's was initially intended for white people suffering during the Great Depression. As in other US cities, Chicago's population began to decline after World War Two. "White flight" to the suburbs was to some extent off-set by a dramatic increase in the city's African-American population, which went from eight per cent in 1940 to 23 per cent (a total of 812,637) in 1960.

Faced with an acute housing shortage, under the enlightened leadership of Elizabeth Wood, CHA attempted to build more decent

Vacant lot, South Side of Chicago.

affordable homes and to integrate them. This provoked violent resistance from white communities in the west of the city and, after Wood was sacked in 1954, a process of selecting sites for much needed public housing based on ethnic profiling. Although this practice was legally prescribed in 1969, the pattern of CHA providing "housing for black people" was established and cannot be disconnected from the pejorative image and iniquitous treatment of the city's public housing.

In the early 1990s, after a series of financial and managerial crises and high-profile violent incidents, CHA embarked on a course that has had profound consequences for the South Side. It has also strongly influenced the future of publicly owned housing throughout the US and, indirectly, the UK. Coming to the spurious conclusion that the many problems of public housing were ultimately related to their construction, CHA began, with HUD support and encouragement, a programme to demolish the high-rise blocks most of its tenants lived in. Two decades later, Chicago's stock of permanent public housing has reduced by two-thirds, from its peak of 43,000. Most of these demolished homes were in the South Side, many of them in the massive State Street Corridor built between 1950 and 1966, including Stateway Gardens and the 4,349-apartment Robert Taylor Homes. Today the only physical evidence of South Side's public housing are numerous empty, grassed-over lots where they once stood. But these convey only a fraction of the destruction wrought to the area. For a radius of three miles, every street features abandoned derelict sites, boarded up homes, weed-strewn, uneven pavements, pot-holed roads and run-down shopping areas. It's almost as though the South Side has been reclaimed by nature, returned to the virgin-soil or new frontier of property developer fantasies.

The Plan for Transformation

How the South Side came to its current condition is a parable of urban regeneration done to, rather than with, a local community. Recalling CASA's maxim from the Bronx – 'Nothing about us, without us, is for us' – Herman Bonner regards the city's treatment of the South Side as a direct attack on the African-American community and argues that changes claiming to improve the area have actually made things worse.

> They knew when they tore the buildings down that they'd displace people. Children have had to move schools, some to suburban areas in the far South Side, so it's a double displacement. The black community's social infrastructure has been destroyed. The demolitions have also disrupted the gang structure. Today the violence is random.

To illustrate his last point, he produces a photo on his phone showing the dead body of a 14-year old boy shot in the street behind Herman's home a few days before we met. It's no more valid to attribute such shocking incidents to contemporary urban policy than it was to post-war public housing, but there is a profound sense that some South Side residents have been abandoned to their fates while the authorities pursue an ideologically-driven clearance policy. The main tool for doing this, since 2000, has been the Plan for Transformation (PfT), described by CHA as:

> ...the most ambitious redevelopment effort of public housing in the United States, with the goal of redeveloping or rehabilitating the entire stock of public housing in Chicago...and (to) strengthen communities by integrating public housing and its leaseholders into the larger social, economic and physical fabric of Chicago.

Building on the practices established by HOPE VI, the objective of PfT has been to replace high-rise public housing with low-rise mixed income housing. But as with other initiatives of its type, in the US and UK, replacement entails a fundamental, though surreptitious, restructuring of non-market housing options. PfT was originally due for completion in 2015 and has cost over $1 billion. Progress has been retarded by the crash in the property market which, perversely, is presented by the authorities as the source of public housing's salvation! The swathes of vacant land are testimony to a policy gone badly wrong.

Unusually, CHA has attempted to track the movements of the 16,500[75] households who lived in public housing at the outset of PfT, all of whom were promised a "right to return". In practice, this was denied to 28 per cent of them. At the end of 2010, 56 per cent (9,388 families) remained in the CHA system, 44 per cent had moved without trace, died or been evicted. Of those still receiving CHA assistance, 44 per cent were in receipt of a housing voucher that effectively moved them into the private rented sector. Only 20 per cent of former CHA tenants included in the research had been accepted for new mixed income housing. CHA dispute the sugges-

---

[75] This was a limited sample from a total of 26,000 CHA households originally affected by the PfT. See CHA *The Plan for Transformation: An update on relocation*, April 2011.

tion that former residents have been moved away from the inner-city South Side area, but their figures indicate otherwise. Of the 3,395 residents CHA surveyed who were still living in public housing, 75 per cent had remained in their original localities. But of former public housing households who are now voucher holders, a higher proportion were living further afield in more isolated neighbourhoods.

Detailed research by a coalition of Illinois housing advocates[76] found that CHA's "aggressive" use of vouchers was reinforcing ethnic discrimination by reducing choice and driving low-income families into more expensive private renting. The Urban Institute[77] also evaluated the results of PfT and found that while most CHA residents who moved to new homes felt their housing conditions had got better, this did not necessarily translate to an overall improvement in their quality of life. That large-scale, expensive regeneration programmes can build apparently better quality homes has often been used as cover for their inability to address more deep-rooted social problems. Such schemes stand accused by campaigners of doing nothing to really tackle poverty, only of moving it around.

Leah Levinger from the Chicago Housing Initiative campaign believes the Plan for Transformation represents an attritional programme of displacement and deconcentration of poor, black households, putting demolition before rehousing, and that part of the intention was "to create a level of turmoil that prevented a community response".

The Plan for Transformation is incomplete, behind schedule and has highly contentious outcomes. Yet CHA is embarking on its next wave of divestment, an application under the new HUD Rental Assistance Demonstration (RAD) programme that could reduce its stock by another 11,000 homes. It remains to be seen how much

---

[76] *Are We Home Yet?: Creating real choice for housing choice voucher families in Chicago*, IHARP, 2010.

[77] *CHA Residents and the Plan for Transformation*, Urban Institute, January 2013.

genuinely affordable housing will be produced by RAD in Chicago, but there is evidence of the expedience that drives such policies. Other PHAs (including Boston, New York and Jersey City) use financial necessity to justify their assorted plans for deconstructing, restructuring and privatising public housing. That argument doesn't wash in Chicago. At the end of 2013, the CHA had a surplus of at least $440 million, including government subsidies for its 2,800 empty homes (one third of those at Altgeld Gardens, where Barack Obama used to work). This was at a time when there were 280,000 people on the waiting list.[78]

Public housing – "Done as a concept"?

Chicago graphically exposes the fundamental issues facing US public housing, with strong and growing echoes for council housing in the UK. A series of inter-linking, superficial judgments about The Projects or Estates are used to establish a narrative of political justification for their destruction. Clichés depicting "disaster", "dependency" and "delinquency" are trailed through the media and become the stuff of common-sense understandings. A host of so-called experts are summoned to prescribe solutions to problems that are, at most, symptomatic rather than causally related. Invariably the resulting policies are informed by commercial vested interests. They rarely reflect the views of tenants themselves, who are seen as incapable of making their own decisions, particularly in the context of increasing alienation from and non-participation in mainstream electoral politics.

During and after World War Two, Chicago engaged in the mass provision of public housing on a similar scale to the UK in the same period. Facing a housing crisis, direct public investment enabled the construction of tens of thousands of good quality homes in both places. The designs were not monolithic. Chicago public housing of the period consisted of a mix of low, medium and high-rise build-

---

[78] The CHA waiting list was actually closed, so this is an underestimate.

ings similar to many post-war UK council estates, and far more representative of municipal housing in both countries than tower blocks. But from the early 1950s, in both the US and UK there was a significant shift away from more varied development. Again, the explanations for this are more complex than the stereotypes allow. Popular prejudice ascribes it to an infatuation with the architecture of Le Corbusier, blended with big State or even communist sympathies. This overlooks the humanistic and design qualities of "non-traditional" housing, much of which has stood the test of time. It also ignores the role of the private construction industry in an unholy alliance with local politicians seeking a quick fix to their housing problems. Patrick Dunleavy[79] vividly describes how this played out in the UK where unscrupulous developers gorged on government subsidies for building high, but not well. Dunleavy explains how the management of council housing on a mass scale quickly became unwieldy, inefficient and excessively bureaucratic. The dynamics of post-war public housing growth in the US were different. The political imperative was to house an impoverished black community in cities that were being drained of their economic base by suburban flight, at a time when segregation was still the norm. For the real estate industry, public housing represented both an opportunity and a threat. While securing lucrative contracts to build public housing, developers could use public housing to contain those they wanted to exclude from the suburbs. In Chicago and other US cities, public housing has never been allowed to threaten the market domination of the private real estate industry.

The ultimate example of this policy dynamic is the Pruitt-Igoe development in St Louis, whose demolition in 1972, 18 years after construction, came to symbolise for some the failure of public housing. In fact an array of systemic problems made success almost impossible. A similar cause celebre in the UK, the partial collapse

---

[79] Dunleavy P (1981) *The Politics of Mass Housing in Britain, 1945 – 75: Study of corporate power and political influence in the welfare state*, Oxford, Oxford University Press.

of the Ronan Point tower block in 1968, causing four deaths, distorted the perception of council housing, though it was largely the result of cost-cutting by profit-driven building contractors.

No-one who has ever lived and/or worked in public or council housing pretends it's perfect. Mismanagement, inefficiency, negligence, paternalism, political patronage, corruption, crime and violence are all real problems. But as one former CHA tenant puts it "Bad things happen in public housing, but bad things happen everywhere".

The casual stigmatisation of public and council housing ignores their intrinsic and lasting benefits. Homes were built at a speed and quality the private sector could and would not match, particularly in times of crisis. Direct municipal investment has achieved intergenerational stability to working class communities on a scale that is often unrecognised. While some, including some housing campaigners, argue that public housing is "done as a concept", this is contradicted by the many thousands of Americans who want to live in it and the corresponding 1.8 million UK households currently on waiting lists for council housing.

From Chicago to Carpenters

After 35 years of systematic denigration and disinvestment, Chicago-type processes are arriving in the UK, albeit on a smaller scale. The London Borough of Newham has 18,000 families on its waiting list, but in 2008 it declared it "had enough social housing". In 2012, Newham council began to empty the 700-home Carpenters Estate in Stratford, east London. It planned to demolish the estate and sell the land to a university interested in building a campus near the Olympic Park. When the deal fell through, Newham left the homes empty, hoping another suitor would emerge. Familiar arguments about the physical condition of tower blocks were used to justify this move, but it met determined resistance from residents and the Focus E15 campaign – some of whose members were faced with displacement. This eventually forced an apology from the Mayor of Newham and the promise of partial re-population of the estate. However, the threat of redevelopment has not been lifted and Carpenters blocks remain empty. Numerous other council estates in London and across the UK face a similar threat, particularly in the wake of the Housing and Planning Act 2016, which facilitates the use of public land for private house building. The constant variable, as in the US, is non-market housing occupying valuable land where developers want to build private apartments and politicians and to alter the social demographic.

A morning in housing court

Another aspect of Chicago's urban malaise is found at an imposing city centre building named after Richard J Daley, the powerful long-time Mayor who oversaw the mass public housing programme of the 1950s and 1960s. The housing court of Cook County is known by campaigners as "eviction court", with good reason. Within half an hour of opening at 9.30am on a damp morning in early June 2015, I witnessed 20 eviction orders granted against tenants who weren't there to defend themselves, or had been unable to pay a lawyer to represent them. Tenants have no "right to counsel" so the power imbalance is further shifted in favour of the property owner. One landlord was seeking to evict a tenant because she had sworn at him! The judicial production line of uncontested eviction orders usually silences the stories of those on the receiving end of them. One case that was heard that morning illustrates the brutality and dehumanisation wrought by the housing crisis.

A landlord, represented by an attorney like a character from a John Grisham novel, was claiming possession for rent arrears between $7,000 and $10,000. The landlord wasn't sure exactly how much he was owed, something a defence attorney might have seized on to discredit the case. But the tenant couldn't afford a lawyer and was represented by his daughter. When the tenant, a disabled Vietnam veteran, moved in, the landlord suggested they set up a joint bank account so the tenant's pension could be paid directly to cover the $2,000 per month rent. Again, a lawyer would probably have questioned the legitimacy of this arrangement, but with an acute housing shortage, tenants are easily exploited. The tenant and his partner were joined in the home by their daughter and her four children, meaning the house was overcrowded. The rent proved unaffordable, but the tenants also complained that the landlord had failed to carry out repairs and of severe mould and sewage backing up into the bath. The landlord claimed the tenant was dipping into the shared account which, the daughter pointed out, only contained her father's money, some of which he needed to pay for medicine. The family claimed they also made cash rent payments, but there was no rent book or other accounting system so this became their word against the landlord's. A lawyer might have asked if the landlord was also withdrawing money from the shared account. He eventually admitted to taking the $1,500 that would have paid for the tenant's legal representation. The home the landlord was so desperate to repossess is in a gentrifying area. He was prepared to waive the thousands of dollars he was supposedly owed in order to get the tenants out. Despite the daughter's best efforts and the apparent sympathy of the judge, the family were given 30 days to leave.

In his vivid, powerful account of the housing crisis in Milwaukee, Matthew Desmond describes a morning in eviction court that closely matches my experience in Chicago:

> When tenants did not show up and their landlord or a representative did, the caller applied three quick stamps to the file – indicating that the tenant had received a default eviction judgment – and placed it on top of a growing pile. The sound of eviction court was a soft hum of dozens of people sighing, coughing, murmuring, and whispering to children, interspersed with the cadence of a name, a pause, and three loud thumps of the stamp.[80]

---

[80] Desmond M (2016) *Evicted: Poverty and profit in the American city* (p 96 – 97), London, Allen Lane.

Evictions in the US rose sharply between 2008 and 2011, reaching a peak of 3.9 million before falling back to 3.4 million in 2014. It's a clear sign of the city's housing turmoil that Chicago leads the nation with 20,572 evictions in 2014 down from a peak of 32,231 in 2012. In England and Wales, 170 tenants a day lost their homes in 2015, a record annual high of 42,728 and a 53 per cent increase over five years.[81] According to figures from the Ministry of Justice in 2015, 19,000 evictions were by council or housing association landlords, 22,000 by private landlords of which approximately 16,000 were through the "accelerated procedure" enabling mandatory evictions of tenants with Assured Shorthold Tenancies.

Millions of American and British tenants are losing their homes as landlords hike rents with impunity. But one of the clear intentions of US and UK housing policy is to move more people – and particularly poor people – out of the relative security of the public sector and into the precarious, parasitic private rented sector. This is implicit in the range of measures being used to destabilise permanent non-market housing, with one dubious concept repeatedly used as the rationale.

Mixed motives

Mixed Income development assumes additional resonance in Chicago because one of the key epithets used to validate the wholesale destruction of its public housing is that it had become "housing for poor people". Policy slogans of "poverty ghettos", "underclass" and "mono-culture", some of which originated in Chicago, rest upon a biased, pathological and ahistorical interpretation of non-market housing and working class communities. In both the US and UK, the ideological roots of public/council housing explicitly embraced the objective of building socially mixed neighbourhoods, and in both countries this was achieved, to a degree. The class composition

---

[81] "Tenant evictions reach highest level on record", *The Guardian*, 12th February 2016.

and political cultures of capitalist economies have altered significantly since the early-mid 20th century, but Aneurin Bevan's[82] vision for council housing could equally have been shared by Elizabeth Wood in Chicago:

> We should try to introduce in our modern villages and towns what was always the lovely feature of English and Welsh villages, where the doctor, the grocer, the butcher and the farm labourer all lived in the same street. I believe that is essential for the full life of a citizen... to see the living tapestry of a mixed community.

But Bevan was also prophetically aware of the causes and dangers of polarised housing provision:

> Consider the grave civic damage caused by allowing local authorities to build homes for only the lower income groups and private speculators to build homes for the higher income groups...you have castrated communities...colonies of low income people living in houses provided by local authorities and higher income groups living in their own colonies...[this] is a monstrous infliction upon the essential psychological and biological one-ness of the community.[83]

The key question, in Chicago and elsewhere, is how we deviated from the first statement and arrived at the second? The answer lies in examining the essence of our system for organising housing and the unequal treatment of different groups within it. In their insightful article, James DeFilippis and Jim Fraser get to the heart of why mixed income has become so prevalent, but also make a more general point about how housing policy is shaped:

> ...(mixed income) is based on the (hegemonic) mantra that low income people themselves are the problem, and that a benevolent gentry needs to colonise their home space in order to create the condi-

---

[82] The post-war Labour government's Minister for Health who, significantly, also had responsibility for housing.
[83] Hansard, Vol. 414, 17th October 1945.

tions necessary to help the poor 'bootstrap' themselves into a better socioeconomic position.[84]

The "benevolent gentry" is as alive and well today as it was when Sidney Waterlow espoused his "wisest plan" for housing policy in the 1870s (see p4-5). Chicago's public housing developed alongside successive attempts by people with more political power to determine and profit from the living conditions of those with less. CHA moved from providing emergency housing for working class whites and demobbed GIs, via a period of ethnically integrated model housing, to "welfare housing" overwhelmingly occupied by African-Americans, Latinos, the disabled and the elderly. Other PHAs developed in like fashion and UK council housing is following a similar path. But these transitions were the result of deliberate policies responding to the failures, bias and manipulation of the housing market. The alleged panacea of mixed income is but the latest attempt to mediate, mitigate and manage the irreconcilable tensions between the interests of private property and those of public well-being with decent homes for all. Herman Bonner's reaction to mixed income housing is "I've never understood how living next door to a rich person benefits me".

The housing profession knows best
Firmly embedded within the mixed income narrative is the tradition of paternalism that has been associated with trans-Atlantic housing policy and management since it emerged as a reputed "profession". Many of the first housing managers were women, schooled in the benevolent but morally judgmental Victorian tradition of Octavia Hill, inherited by Jane Addams and Elizabeth Wood in Chicago and continuing to influence housing practice elsewhere, even as it has become increasingly male-dominated. One of the core beliefs within the philanthropic housing credo is that "good" behaviour by some will be imitated by others. One of the most influ-

---

[84] DeFilippis and Fraser (2010) "Why Do We Want Mixed-Income Housing Neighbourhoods?" (p136), in *Critical Urban Studies*.

ential propagators of this view in the US was Vince Lane, a former CHA Director, who in 1995 wrote:

> Redefining the responsibilities of PHAs will make breaking down the walls of public housing's isolation from other communities an achievable goal...Most important, the community will include a socio-economically mixed population providing children with healthy role models and encouraging adults to improve their own lives and the lives of their families.[85]

Mr Lane toured the UK with this message. Six years later, he was convicted of fraud and sent to prison! But while Lane's personal tragedy may be exceptional, his views are not. In the UK, a systematic accretion of political and media messages has been linking council/social housing to allegedly problematic forms of behaviour for many years. This has grown in momentum alongside attempts to privatise the remaining non-market stock. The Centre for Social Justice (CSJ) has been an influential policy think-tank for post-2010 UK government policy. It was set up by a former Conservative Party leader, Iain Duncan-Smith, following an apparent epiphany during an extended visit to a deprived Scottish council estate. Invoking a parade of folk devils and symbols of moral panic, under a heading "Social housing – incubating social breakdown" a 2009 CSJ report argues,

> ...social housing is now home to some of our most disadvantaged and vulnerable individuals and families...The majority of social housing households are now headed by young, workless lone parents and single men and women...Gangs are, unsurprisingly, most commonly found in these highly deprived areas...Alongside [these] social economic changes has been the breakdown of the family unit...The lack of positive male role models has meant that the masculinity being modelled to gang-involved young men is that of a hyper-alpha male.[86]

---

[85] Lane V (1995) "Best Management Practices in US Public Housing", in *Housing Policy Debate*, Vol. 5, issue 4.

[86] "Dying to Belong", *CSJ*, February 2009.

In another report, the CSJ approvingly quotes the Mayor of Newham, in east London, the authority that emptied the Carpenters Estate:

> ...we allocate properties on the basis of how you present yourself to a local council, so if you walk in and say 'I'm homeless' you get a greater priority than if you walk in and say 'I've managed to do something for myself but I'm still looking for a council property'. And so the whole way we allocate is unfair, it doesn't necessarily enable us to support aspiration.[87]

Mr Duncan-Smith sums up the CSJ's attitude to council and social housing:

> Many areas of social housing are blighted by fractured families, worklessness, educational failure, addictions, serious personal debt, anti-social behaviour and crime. Too many tenants find themselves on estates where welfare dependency is a way of life...
> (Speech at Institute of Housing conference, June 2008)

With little if any evidence, an almost identical narrative of judgementalism and personal morality has evolved around UK council/social housing as that used to justify the virtual destruction of Chicago and US public housing – and with the same aim.

From El Salvador to Chicago

Maite Quevedo provides a special insight on Chicago's housing plight. She arrived in the city to escape the civil war in her own country, studied to become an urban planner and now works for a tenant advocacy and organising campaign. Asked if she's happy to be in the USA, Maite replies "I don't think immigrants ever resolve that question" and continues:

> Immigrants are the new slaves in America. They're discriminated against in so many ways. A big chunk of the low-income renters in the

---

[87] "Housing Poverty: From social breakdown to social mobility", *CSJ*, November 2008.

North Side right now are Latinos and that's where there's big competition for housing, because that's where whites are coming back to the
city from the suburbs.

A lot of current attention on America's urban conflict focuses
on the African-American community, particularly in the aftermath of the Ferguson unrest and the Black Lives Matter
campaign. These struggles have largely over-shadowed those of
the Latino population, some relatively recent immigrants from
rural communities. This contrast sometimes plays out in inter-
ethnic rivalry within Chicago civil rights campaigns, which Maite
succinctly describes as "fighting over the crumbs while somebody
else has the pie".

Chicago's 900,000 Latinos[88] are approximately 30 per cent of
the city's population. People from Latin and Central America are
spread throughout the city, with the highest concentrations in the
north just beyond the commercial district. This is an area of intense
developer activity, gentrification and displacement symbolised by
the clearance (1995 – 2011) of the 3,600 home Cabrini-Green
housing development. Latinos were and remain less likely to live
in public housing so are not victims of the Plan for Transformation
on the same scale as African-Americans. But as private renters they
are constantly threatened by owners converting buildings to more
lucrative condominiums.[89] Approximately half the Chicago Latino
population rent privately, the proportion increasing as income
decreases, and the poorest are particularly exposed to the city's
worst housing conditions. They have not had equal access to more
affordable, non-market alternatives. Only half of Latinos who
quality for CHA assistance because of their low income, either

---

[88] This is an uncomfortable generalising term, but one that Maite was happy to use. The
vast majority of Latino Chicagoans (80 per cent) are from Mexico, followed by people from
Puerto Rico (ten per cent), Cuba and other central American nations.

[89] "Condo" apartment blocks in the US roughly translate to a private block of leasehold flats in
the UK. Condo Conversion has become synonymous with speculative property development
and the erosion of more affordable housing for people with low or medium incomes.

through public housing or vouchers, actually receive it. As Maite explains, this discrimination is reinforced by CHA's failure to issue the housing vouchers for which they receive federal funding, instead "sitting on the money" that could help another 13,000 families a year. Taken together with CHA's hoarding of surpluses from its other operations, Maite is in no doubt that the entire organisation, or what remains of it, is being "fattened up for privatisation".

With the brutality of eviction court in mind, Maite describes the appalling conditions, spiralling rents and constant threat of eviction experienced by poor Latinos in Chicago. After the 2008 crash, many landlords are either struggling to pay for the upkeep of or deliberately running down buildings, removing low-income tenants and replacing them with those able to pay higher rents, or selling to speculative property investors. This process is at work throughout the inner-city, with two tides of redevelopment encroaching on working class areas from north and south. This pincer movement is partly being driven by the University of Chicago and the Obama Foundation, both gobbling up land and fuelling displacement. The development frenzy is pushing up land values and rents. Month-to-month and neighbourhood-to-neighbourhood rent levels in Chicago, like any other place, vary, but the overall trend is clear. Chicago became a "rent burdened" city in 2012 when the median rent exceeded 30 per cent of median income and although un-affordability hasn't reached the stratospheric levels of New York or San Francisco, Chicago rents continue to rise.

Maite reflects on the changes to her city as another derelict factory on East 18th Street was being torn down to make way for another block of luxury apartments. As she said, we are witnessing long term changes to the character of cities and as in New York and London a key feature is the pricing out of low and medium income households. Cities are getting richer and whiter, suburbs are getting poorer and more ethnically mixed. More Latinos now live in Chicago's far-flung suburbs, a change that reflects a relocation of poverty as much as any aspirational move to leafy environs. At the start of the 2000s, 60 per cent of the Chicago area's poverty was inside the city limits. A decade later it was half that, but poverty in DeKalb County, 50 miles west of the city, had risen steeply. In Maite's words, Chicago has become "a glittering city at the core with its skirts all torn at the edges".

Fighting the machine

In 2015, a city long associated with machine politics and boss mayors was shaken. Jesus "Chuy" Garcia, a Mexican immigrant with a background in housing campaigns and a programme of reform, challenged incumbent Rahm Emanuel (a close ally of President Obama) to become Mayor of Chicago. As a rank outsider, Garcia won 34 per cent of the February vote, forcing an April run-off in which he lost but gained 44 per cent of the vote. In Maite's view, Emanuel "basically bought the election". His campaign budget of $16 million dwarfed Garcia's $2 million, a reminder of the bloated financing of the American political process that has yet to fully reach British shores. Garcia emphasised housing in his campaign. His policies spoke directly to the city's housing crisis and, among other things, advocated direct public investment in genuinely affordable homes within a more transparent and accountable Chicago Housing Authority, and a strategy that linked "fair housing for all" to transport, health, education and the environment. Garcia connected with the radical, progressive tradition of Chicago politics, anticipating later high-profile national campaigns by Bernie Saunders in the US and Jeremy Corbyn in the UK, in which housing emerged from the political backwater. For Maite, the essence of the housing crisis is simple: "We focus on tenant v landlord conflicts, but the real cause is people don't have enough money".

Conclusion

From a British perspective, the scars on Chicago's urban landscape are shocking. It's a class war zone. The South Side symbolises the subjugation of a working class community by those with economic and political power to control the city. Estimates of the number of people displaced by two decades of Chicago's urban policy vary from 70,000 to 200,000, the overwhelming majority of them African-Americans. These figures are inherently unreliable and mask the variety of reasons why people may have left. But allowing for the "pull" as well as the "push", the volume of suburban migration in Chicago and other US cities is structurally transforming them and American society on an historic scale.

4

Seattle: Logging in, logged out

Introduction

Seattle, in the state of Washington on America's majestic Pacific Northwest coast, was once a centre for the logging industry and a staging post for the Klondike gold rush. Today it's a centre for high-tech industries: the literal birthplace of Microsoft (in the form of Bill Gates), Amazon and their ubiquitous liquid accompaniment, Starbucks. With its spectacular natural setting, Seattle has come to signify metropolitan cultural chic, the urbanity of Frasier blending with the edginess of Nirvana. It has been described as a "city of the future", strangely embodied by the Space Needle, a 1960s folly resembling (and perhaps inspiring) a building from the Jetsons cartoon. But Seattle is also a boom and bust city. From the gold-rush and timber trade to the collapse of Washington Mutual bank, then the city's biggest employer, in the aftermath of sub-prime, Seattle has risen and fallen on waves of speculative investment. Today its economy sits on the hope that a circuit of high-tech consumerism will never be broken. All this is reflected in a deeply divided and divisive housing market.

Welcome to Nickelsville

Its official address is 1010 South Dearborn Street, but Nickelsville does not conform to the shiny Seattle image. Wedged between several large roads, on a flinty scrap of waste-ground from a J G Ballard[90] novel, Nickelsville is a camp for some of Seattle's displaced poor. There are half a dozen similar places in the city. Noah, a resident who used to work for Microsoft before mental ill-health forced a reappraisal of his life, explains that Nickelsville is home to 40 people (including some children), victims of Seattle's dysfunctional, overheated housing market. There are also people escaping domestic violence and other forms of abuse, as well as addiction problems. They live in small huts (not much bigger than a typical garden shed)

---

[90] By strange coincidence, there's a district in Seattle called Ballard, where there is also an informal housing settlement.

or tents arranged in neat rows and extending up the hill where Amazon had its first corporate headquarters. Nickelsville is run as a co-operative, with residents working off their rent by shared cleaning, administration and guarding duties. Noah explains that most of his neighbours work, at least part time, but can't afford Seattle rents. He emphasises Nickelsville isn't part of a protest or "occupy" movement, it's a necessity. "It's either this or leave Seattle for who knows what or where."

Nickelsville is only one sign of Seattle's housing crisis. As well as the other organised sites like it, there are people sleeping rough in more or less visible places throughout the city. Every evening, hundreds gather in the downtown area around City Hall, where there are several homeless hostels. Tents and improvised shelters dot the city fringe. Homelessness statistics are notoriously unreliable, but a "single night count" for the Seattle area in 2016 recorded 4,505 "unsheltered" homeless, a 19 per cent increase on the previous year and the third highest level in the country. Some sources suggest the real figure is double this. One of the vital remaining differences between the UK and the US is that homeless Americans, including their children, have absolutely no legal right to housing. Statutory provision of shelter may for some seem contrary to a deep sense of self-sufficiency as an intrinsic part of American national identity. But this is also a manipulated ideological tool used to hide policy failings.

The existence of Nickelsville in one of the richest cities of the richest country on earth should be conclusive proof that the housing market doesn't work. But it inspires a range of other reactions. From adversity Noah, his fellow-residents and the thousands of other people shut out of the housing mainstream are making their own arrangements. Such resourcefulness and enterprise are not unique to Americans, but convey a frontier spirit, particularly in a young city like Seattle, which was only settled by Europeans in the 1850s, and a state, Washington, only admitted to the union in 1884. There is something at Nickelsville that echoes the many utopian communities developed in the Seattle area around the turn of the 20th

Nickelsville.

century which helped establish the region's reputation for progressive politics. Like these earlier experimental settlements, Nickelsville has also suffered internal disputes that threatened its future. Ultimately, the biggest threats to Nickelsville residents are the constant possibility that their temporary encampment will be moved on and that "temporary" becomes permanent as the housing crisis persists and deepens.[91]

Kings County, the jurisdiction containing Seattle, unveiled a ten-year plan to end homelessness in 2005, but the numbers continue to grow. Local rents are rising to levels that for most tenants are tantamount to an eviction notice. This was fuelled by a $3.3 billion apartment-buying splurge in 2014, much of it spent by people in the high-tech industry, where average wages are $90,000 and incomes of the richest five per cent grew faster than anywhere else in the US. In mid-2015, there were 42 construction cranes on the Seattle

---

[91] Nickelsville at South Dearborn Street was cleared by the police in March 2016. It has moved to another site in Seattle.

Nickelsville.

skyline, as wealth continues to be embodied in property. Despite some signs that the city's seemingly insatiable appetite for growth was slowing, average house prices increased by 18 per cent in 2015.

Manufactured housing (not "mobile homes")

If homeless people are the most visible sign of America's failing, iniquitous housing policy, there's a bigger, more hidden community belying the image of affluent suburbs or luxury apartments. Almost as stigmatised as public housing residents, but far greater in number, are the estimated 20 million Americans who live in mobile homes. As with other forms of housing outside the mainstream, a range of stereotypes and myths have built up about people who live on trailer parks, in what many prefer to call manufactured housing. There are 8.5 million such homes, 6.4 per cent of the US housing stock. The highest concentrations are in the southern states, with the most in South Carolina where they constitute almost one fifth of residences. Eight per cent of households in Washington State live in manufactured housing. Not all mobile home households are poor and 57 per cent contain someone in full-time employment, but their median income is only about half the national level. Twenty three per cent are retirees and this reflects an element of choice to live in the sector, particularly by "downsizing" or moving to the "sun belt" states, but also the fact that at least one-third of Americans over 65 live in poverty. Like Nickelsville, manufactured housing resonates with a deeper sense of American identity, combining individual resilience with collective solidarity. Manufactured housing, with an average price of $67,000, has become the only route to an afford-able home for many Americans. Approximately one third (3.1 million) of manufactured homes have been added in the last 20 years. The national advocacy group for manufactured housing residents is at pains to emphasise the equal citizenship of its members and does so by invoking quasi-religious American values:

> Among the basic principles fought for by the founding fathers of this country was that of basic property rights. The owner of a manufactured home shares the same tangible investment as does the owner of a one-bedroom condominium or a fifty-room mansion.[92]

Trailer parks (which are located beyond city centres) highlight some important geographic features of US housing and society. Despite being overwhelmingly an urban population, 20 per cent of Americans live in rural areas, another ten per cent in conurbations of less than 50,000 people. The potency of small town, middle-America is widely acknowledged in political terms. It's also essential to recognise that most Americans don't live in the metropolitan areas of the East and West coasts. Settlement patterns are further compli-cated by the increasingly blurred boundaries between urban, subur-ban and rural areas, as new speculative housing spreads beyond city limits and swallows up vast amounts of agricultural land. Sprawl is often depicted as characteristic of wasteful American consumption.

---

[92] "Vision", National Manufactured Home Owners Association website.

But it is also a consequence of people compelled to move further afield before they find a home they can afford. The unbalanced, uncontrolled US economy allows some places to grow exponentially, while others wither and struggle to survive. Big city regions are sucking in people and profits. Smaller, former industrial cities and towns are seeing their populations and economies plummet, issues that came dramatically into focus with the election of Donald Trump.

Champion of the parks

Kylin Parks got involved in housing campaigns in 2008, when her home and 97 others in a manufactured housing community in Lynnwood, 20 miles north of Seattle, was threatened with redevelopment. As Kylin recalls, it was just before the crash and rising land prices meant the site owner could sell for $10 million. Residents of trailer parks usually own their homes, but not the land they sit on. Kylin took a year off from her sales job and launched a campaign to defend her home and community. She organised an owners' group and successfully lobbied the local authority, Snohomish County, to buy the site on the basis that it was a good use of public money to protect and preserve almost 100 homes for low-income seniors. Inspired by victory, Kylin became a full-time tenant organiser for the Washington Tenants Union. As she says, her initial success would not be possible today because of cuts in public finance, and with the speculative property bubble reflating rapidly, many more manufactured housing communities are under threat of displacement.

Kylin is a passionate advocate for the benefits of manufactured homes.[93] She moved to one when she was priced out of Seattle following a divorce.

> I could have my garden and my dog. It was a little piece of heaven when I was rebuilding my life. I love it. It's an amazing community. People care about each other in a way you don't find elsewhere.

---

[93] Some of the more negative aspects of trailer park life are described by Matthew Desmond in *Evicted* (2016).

Kylin is not alone in arguing that manufactured housing should be part of a more rational housing system. The multiple benefits of off-site construction of homes built in factory conditions are widely recognised but under-utilised. In part, this is because it runs counter to the culture and preferences of the private development industry and a number of other vested interests. Manufactured housing also disturbs a widely-held perception of what a "real home" looks like. The iconography of the three-bedroom semi with a front and back garden is as embedded in the American as the British psyche (with some variations of scale). Living in a caravan or trailer, like public and council housing, does not conform with the aspirational ideal of private home ownership. It does not convey the social status and respectability that the property industry thrives on. It was this instinct that Levitt and Sons recognised and exploited on Long Island (p42). They did so by optimising the efficiency of the construction process and thus bringing down costs. Many of the original Levittown houses were little more than mobile homes, although they have been significantly embellished since. Speed and economy were the main aims of the Levitts, not environmental issues, but all these are, or should be, concerns for today's housing policy. Manufactured housing offers a model for building lots of homes quickly and cheaply, while reducing the use of energy and resources in construction and during occupation.

Plotlands, Squatters, Prefabs and Travellers

Trailer parks are a particular feature of US housing, but they have important parallels in the UK. The plotland movement developed in Britain between the late 19th century and the outbreak of the Second World War, combining a new but growing taste for holidays with an older one for land ownership. Working class families, mostly from London, began to buy small, cheap parcels of unused agricultural land and build their own homes. This was a faint echo of the 19th century homestead movement in the US. Initially plotlands were for weekend breaks, but over time developed into permanent communities organised around co-operative development of and responsibility for services and facilities. What were originally wooden shacks became brick-built homes with picket fences. During and after the war, plotland communities became more popular as a refuge from the Blitz and its bomb damage. The largest plotlands were eventually incorporated into the New Town of Basildon, Essex, an assertion of formal State housing and planning policy over the informal self-build arrangements of the plotlanders. But remnants of the original housing can still be seen at Jaywick, Peacehaven and Dungeness on the English south coast.

The post-war UK housing crisis provoked other self-organised responses that challenged establishment property norms. A mass occupation of public land, particularly disused huts on military bases, involved 40,000 homeless people at 1,000 camps across the country. As with the plotlands, some of these temporary shelters eventually became permanent and the movement added huge pressure for the post-war Labour government to prioritise the building of council homes. Squatting of unused or empty buildings has continued to be a feature of campaigns demanding housing justice, and despite moves to criminalise the practice, has continued during the current UK housing crisis. Another innovative policy for tackling the post-1945 housing shortage, with direct similarities to US manufactured housing, was the provision by public authorities of 146,000 'prefabs' – factory built homes that remained for decades. Prefabs were much loved by some residents. But prejudice against non-conventional housing endures, most vividly in the treatment of the UK's 58,000 travellers and gypsies living in 18,500 caravans, many of them on permanent sites. Although there are some legal protections for traveller housing, the brutal 2013 eviction of residents from Dale Farm in Essex again exposed the social disapproval of those wanting to live beyond the clutches of the property market. A further attack on the housing rights of travellers and gypsies is contained in the 2016 Housing and Planning Act.

Seattle – America in microcosm

Nickelsville and manufactured housing are symptomatic of America's chronically-failing housing system, even allowing for a degree of positive choice by some residents. The problem, like the nation, is both vast and heavily shaped by local characteristics and politics. Seattle presents some of the key issues in (relative[94]) microcosm. The volatile dynamics of the housing market are now moulding the area's demography and its social and economic development with greater force than the logging industry did 150 years ago.

With more demand for renting after the subprime mortgage crash combined with the influx of lucrative high-tech jobs and resulting population growth, speculative apartment development in central Seattle is approaching ten times the level of 2011. Although there are some signs of over-supply, 65 per cent of new households in the city are renters. Demand is driving rents up by an average of eight per cent a year (from a relatively low base), with some cases of rents doubling or tripling overnight. Kylin Parks describes "a lot of young people making a lot of money" pursuing a lifestyle that revolves around work. She says this new generation of Seattle-residents finds it harder to establish communal or family roots partly because they move so frequently. This transience, reflecting an increasingly temporary jobs market, is endemic to the private rented market. There is no rent control in Seattle, something Kylin attributes to both local and state-wide political forces:

> There's still a lot of good ol' boys on the City Council, but we're also a property rights oriented state. People tend to think if you own land you should be able to do whatever you want with it.

This restatement of inviolable property rights has to be set in the context of the sharply-contrasting political cultures and housing circumstances within and beyond the city. Although 60 per cent of Washington state's population live in the Seattle metropolitan area,

---

[94] Washington state is larger than England and Wales combined.

there is a substantial constituency, particularly east of the Cascade Mountains, that is largely agricultural and conservative, where "red" means Republican not socialist.[95] Housing issues have a very different resonance across the 70,000 square miles of the state. In August 2015, an average two-bedroom apartment in Seattle cost $2,136 per month to rent, its equivalent in Spokane, 280 miles to the west, was $755. Demands for rent control are growing in Seattle, but some of the political power that could bring such reforms is vested in areas like Spokane, where housing is not an issue with the same urgency. Similar disparities exist in other US states and in the UK where the housing situation in big cities – particularly London – is very different to other parts of the country. In both nations, uneven housing conditions in part explain why the issue is not high on the national political agenda.

Land!

Critical to any understanding of American society, including its housing, is the relationship between the people and the land.[96] Defining episodes in US history have centred around land ownership, from the opening of the frontier and dispossession of Native Americans, to the 1862 Homestead Act and the post-civil war policy decreeing that freed slaves should receive "40 acres and a mule". From the earliest colonial settlement, land ownership has been synonymous with an equally sacrosanct principle – freedom. On the eve of the American Revolution in the 1760s, 70 per cent of what were soon to become known as American citizens owned land. For many it was this possibility that motivated their hazardous migration. Today, the Federal government owns approximately 30 per cent of the land (much of it in national parks and military installations). Of the remainder, 97 per cent is concentrated in the hands of three per cent of the population. *The Magazine of the American*

---

[95] The traditional colours of the US Republican party are red, while the Democratic Party's are blue.

[96] Mackin A (2006) *Americans and their Land: The house built on abundance*, Ann Arbor, University of Michigan Press.

Land Owner appeals to its readers in romantic terms: "Giant timber tracts, endless fields of grain, larger-than-life ranches, these are a few of the ways America's largest landowners make the most of one of our essential freedoms".

Telecommunications magnate John Malone reputedly owns 2,200,000 acres of America (an area about one third the size of the UK). A more grotesque renunciation of the beliefs of Native Americans is hard to imagine.

> What is this you call property? It cannot be the earth, for the land is our mother, nourishing all her children, beasts, birds, fish and all men. The woods, the streams, everything on it belongs to everybody and is for the use of all. How can one man say it belongs only to him?[97]

A similarly unequal distribution of land exists on a smaller scale in the UK. Britain still has an essentially feudal land system[98] with an opaque method of recording ownership that makes it impossible to know exactly who owns what. Some argue that the growth of home ownership has redistributed land, but the holdings of the 7.2 million UK citizens who own their home free of a mortgage are dwarfed by those of an aristocratic elite, amongst which four families own 641,000 acres, about one tenth of the country.

The sheer abundance of land in America makes a number of comparisons with the UK difficult, including the dangers of over-development. A persistent myth is that Britain is a "crowded island" in danger of being "concreted over". In fact no more than 15 per cent of UK land is developed. Nonetheless, those seeking to either restrict house building or suggest that the UK doesn't have enough space for more people, particularly foreigners, repeatedly cite dangers of over-development. The blending of environmental and racist arguments with paranoia about property prices exerts significant influence over UK housing policy. While all of these issues

---

[97] Massasoit, leader of the Wampanoag people, c 1581 - 1661
[98] Technically, the whole country is owned by the Crown, sub-divided by various types of tenanted, leased and freehold interests.

have their US equivalent, they don't have the same purchase in a country of 3.5 million square miles and an average density of 96 people per square mile, compared to the average 660 people in each of the UK's 94,000 square miles.

Yesler Terrace

Predictably, within Seattle's tempestuous housing market is a story of access to decent, secure, affordable housing denied. In the heart of downtown, opposite City Hall and a ten-minute walk from Nickelsville, is Yesler Terrace where, until 2014, there were 561 homes owned by the Seattle Housing Authority (SHA). They were built in 1941 and a shaky SHA promotional film of the time ("It Happened on Yesler's Hill") describes the idealistic vision behind Seattle's first public housing:

> Its value lies both in dollars and human happiness...a new pattern of living has arisen out of a slum, made up of sun and space, safety and convenience, privacy and community pride.

These blandishments conceal a more complex history. Unlike other parts of Seattle, the central district was not subject to restrictive covenants that preserved "whites only" neighbourhoods. Before the SHA redevelopment, Yesler Hill was a collection of ramshackle wooden buildings owned by private landlords who exploited an impoverished but ethnically diverse population, including a Japanese community that would soon be deported to internment camps. Like London's Boundary Estate in 1900 – and every large-scale urban improvement project since – access to the new homes at Yesler Terrace was circumscribed by a selection process that aimed at demographic remodelling. SHA stipulated that their first tenants should be US citizens and families headed by married couples, thereby excluding a substantial number of the area's former residents. However, in two respects Yesler Terrace was significantly different to other new public housing. The design was not standard brick-built tenement blocks, but Scandinavian-inspired two-storey terraced homes with front and back gardens, very similar to much post-war UK council housing. Second, the progressive leader of SHA Jesse Epstein (who was later a victim of the McCarthy witch-hunts) insisted that Yesler Terrace would be the first ethnically integrated public housing in the US. This ethno-cultural mix survived for the next half century. In a place often portrayed as a "white city", Yesler Terrace has been described as "the ghetto that wasn't",[99] where African-American, Chinese, east African, Vietnamese and Native American households lived alongside an unusually high proportion of white public housing tenants. What this diverse community had in common was low income: 86 per cent of residents earned below the area AMI. Yesler Terrace gave them an opportunity to live in the city centre, close to service sector jobs, and thus avoid the increasingly long, costly and onerous commutes endured by other workers unable to find housing they could afford in central Seattle.

"A vibrant new community"

Using wearily formulaic language, in the mid-2000s, SHA began a process it intended would lead to the demolition of Yesler Terrace and its replacement, at a cost of $300 million, with a "dynamic mixed income community". In place of two-storey row houses, the 30 acre site will accommodate a litany of features from the 21st century urban policy playbook, including a tenfold increase in residential density (from 500 low rise houses to 5,000 apartments in medium-rise blocks) and almost a million square feet of "mixed use" space. The redevelopment is being sponsored through the HUD Choice Neighbourhoods programme, that has led to the moth-balling of Montgomery Gardens in Jersey City (see p61-62). SHA is gerrymandering the allocation of new homes to skew provision towards higher-earning households, with those on lower

---

[99] "The Twilight of Yesler Terrace: The end of the ghetto that wasn't", Charles Mudede in *The Stranger*, 6th February 2013.

incomes offered the "choice" of a housing voucher that takes them away from Yesler Terrace, while technically maintaining the HUD promise of "one for one" replacement. A striking aspect of the SHA plan is its private sector development partner, Vulcan Inc. This is a multi-purpose, multi-national conglomerate run by Paul G Allen, the 51st richest person in the world and co-founder of Microsoft, who has $17.5 billion in his bank account! Allen has a reputation for philanthropy, but as so often with that practice, it may not be entirely altruistic. Not only will Vulcan Inc. receive the benefit of $30 million in public money from HUD, but it will acquire development rights for a substantial and extremely valuable site in central Seattle, while polishing their public image.

"Renewing Yesler's promise"

SHA has made three commitments about the new housing at Yesler Terrace: there will be "like for like" replacement of public housing, there will be more housing for low income households on site, and all former residents will have a right to return. Given the projected time scale of the redevelopment (15-20 years), these reassurances can be taken, at best, only on trust. But the fact that they have been made – and broken – on numerous occasions elsewhere, makes tenants and campaigners understandably wary. As Sharon Lee from the Low Income Housing Initiative says, even if SHA pledges are met, many former residents are likely to be "lost through the shuffle". Given the slicing and dicing of the new housing mix at Yesler Terrace, this appears inevitable:

Total homes	*5000*
"Extremely low income" units (30 per cent or less AMI) (*Replacement units 561, additional units 100*)	*661*
"Very low income units" (60 per cent or less AMI)	*290*
"Workforce units" (80 per cent AMI)	*850*
Market rate units	*3,200*

With 64 per cent of the new homes at full market rates beyond their means, the attention of former Yesler Terrace tenants and the other 48,000 Seattle residents earning less than 30 per cent of AMI will focus on the remaining 36 per cent. Within the "affordable" new homes already completed are the 120 at "Anthem on 12th", where living is marketed as "a revolutionary experience in the perfect venue" and two bedroom apartments are advertised for $2,125 – $2,250 per month. The maximum genuinely affordable rent (at 30 per cent of income) for Seattle residents earning even 80 per cent (never mind 30 per cent) of AMI is $1,481. Clearly, Anthem on 12th is not intended for the likes of them!

There are further doubts about the true nature of the replacement public housing at Yesler Terrace. Only 420 of the "extremely low income" homes will be on site, although the remaining 141 should be near-by. But as the Seattle Displacement Coalition contends, given the scale of the Yesler Terrace project, only one in ten of the new homes need to be reintegrated as public housing within the scheme to fully achieve SHA's commitment to "like for like" replacement. Furthermore, SHA concedes that some of the additional low-income homes will be developed by "non-profit partners" who will be granted land ownership. Access for tenants will be via housing choice vouchers, another example of the replacement of permanent public housing with vouchers. Even if SHA keeps its promises, the redeveloped Yesler Terrace will be dominated by the remaining 86 per cent of new homes, most of them controlled by Vulcan Inc. Site plans make it clear that any non-market housing will be peripheral and low-income tenants separated from private owners, a form of tenure segregation that contradicts pious claims of a "mixed-income community", but is in keeping with prevailing SHA (and US/UK national) policy. As a Seattle community newspaper comments:

> SHA continues to pursue a policy of systematically replacing public housing with mixed-income developments. Since 1995, SHA has used federal funds to tear down more than 2,000 such units; less than half

were ever replaced. The agency with a mission to serve the city's poorest has become Seattle's biggest destroyer of housing for this group. It's now in the process of doing the same thing at Yesler Terrace.[100]

Consulted or insulted?

The crucial aim for tenants and campaigners in the face of schemes like Yesler Terrace is to establish the right to return, not just as a slogan but as a specific, meaningful and enforceable obligation. This is rarely achieved. Developers and government agencies have become masters of sophistry when presenting residents with seductive arguments for regeneration. This includes dissembling about the exact nature – in terms of tenure and rents – of replacement homes, disguising the full impact of redevelopment within multiple project phases and making empty promises. The mechanism for delivering these messages is "consultation", a word that has become as devalued as "affordable" in the lexicon of 21st century US and UK housing policy.

The consultation process at Yesler Terrace began in 2005. At first SHA denied the scope and extent of its plans and, in another common ploy, accused campaigners warning about displacement of "scare mongering". Part of the anxiety was based on the experience of previous SHA redevelopment projects which lead to a net loss of 1,000 public housing units, a deficit SHA claims was filled with "off site" provision. To combat opposition, SHA developed what Professor James Throgmorton[101] refers to as "persuasive story telling" whereby key themes are invoked to generate support for redevelopment. Such hagiographic texts have traversed the Atlantic and become endemic. They particularly appeal to notions of community and sustainability, touchstone issues in contemporary

---

[100] "Yesler Terrace demolition a sad end to city's legacy of public housing", *Queen Anne and Magnolia Times*, 10th March 2015.

[101] Throgmorton J (2003) *Planning as Persuasive Storytelling in a Global-Scale Web of Relationships* in Planning Theory, Vol. 2(2) pp 125 – 151.

urban policy that have become almost unquestionable. The following two almost inter-changeable examples illustrate the point:

> ...what is being created here is no less than a new, coherent community,
> offering a better and more intelligent way of life. A community that
> combines the lessons learned of the past and the most advanced technol-
> ogy of the present, that conserves our natural resources rather than
> depletes them, that offers the world a blueprint for how life will be lived
> in the future. ("Vision" for Greenwich Millennium Village, south London.)

> ...the new community goes beyond replacement of the housing stock.
> It imagines a place where people live in healthier housing that is part
> of a wider, healthier community – a place where the renewed physical
> environment is matched by strong social connections, access to
> education and economic opportunity. ("Vision" for Yesler Terrace.)

These motifs are buttressed during the consultation process by
glossy brochures and (increasingly) multi-media materials that seek
to establish a virtual reality of a new environment before it has actually been built (use of the word "imagines" above is significant).
Alongside this positive message there is always a negative one. All
projects like Yesler Terrace start with a threat. Often the rationale
for redevelopment, as at Yesler, is couched in technical terms and
focuses on the condition of homes which are claimed to be beyond
economic repair. The detailed information upon which such judgements are made is rarely, if ever, shared with tenants. The commission, consumption and selective exchange of specialist knowledge
is a fundamental and lucrative part of contemporary housing policy.
An entire industry has developed around "consultation", underlin-
ing the inherent inequality in the development process. Authorities
like SHA attempt to control what information is shared with residents and their scope to voice opinions and concerns.

The stock transfer programme in the UK produced numerous
examples of local councils and housing associations hand-picking
compliant consultative forums, marginalising dissenting voices and

actively preventing (and sometimes intimidating) expressions of opposition, for example by refusing speaking rights or ripping down off message posters.

Underlying these manoeuvres is the constant warning that available funding will be withdrawn if residents oppose regeneration, leaving them to suffer in sub-standard homes. Other inducements are offered as collateral benefits from housing redevelopment, in the form of community facilities and infrastructure improvements, but again with the heavily implied threat that these are conditional on acquiescence. Finally, the planning and consultation phases of big housing projects are wrapped within an enormous volume of byzantine documentation and carried out over a prolonged time period, exhausting the limited resources of community groups.

Stepping Forward

The latent intent behind plans for Yesler Place was exposed in August 2014 when SHA announced its Stepping Forward initiative which envisaged "employment services support and new rent policies for work-able adults" living in SHA homes. Couched in the paternalistic language of "self-sufficiency" and justified by dubious claims of promoting fairness and increasing affordable housing, what Stepping Forward amounted to was steep incremental rent rises up to market levels. For example, SHA tenants living in a four-bedroom home could see their rents rise from $180 to $1,060 a week over a period of six years.[102]

Stepping Forward continued a long policy trend in the US and one that is increasingly being exported to the UK, most recently and significantly in the 2016 Housing and Planning Act. Access to US public housing has always been related to income, unlike in the UK where there has been strong resistance to means testing. Since its inception, the US government and local PHAs worked to ensure that public housing was never seen as anything other than "housing

---

[102] See http://seattlehousing.org/about/steppingforward/

for poor people". Their most basic method has been to impose income limits to control both entrance to and exit from the system. Put simply, you cannot become a public housing tenant unless your income is below a certain level and you have to leave if it rises above a certain level. The mythologised figure of the "millionaire council tenant" was never allowed to be even a possibility in the US.[103]

For policy makers and politicians the ostensible concern is that people they deem can afford not to, will live in "subsidised" housing. The embedded fallacies in the presentation of how different forms of tenure are subsidised underpins the wider bias against any form of non-market housing. Owner occupation is habitually portrayed as free of government subsidy and therefore an expression of personal independence, in contrast to the "dependency" of non-market renting. The reality is that throughout the history of US and UK housing policy, private housing has been far more heavily subsidised than public sector alternatives. This, however, is not the message that Stepping Forward trades on. It and similar initiatives thrive on the stereotype of indigent and indolent tenants as targeted in Bill Clinton's 1996 Personal Responsibility and Work Opportunity Reconciliation Act. Clinton's "bootstrap" theory linked poor people and access to welfare benefits via a set of moralistic judgments which, in the US context, are visited upon public housing tenants in particular. A very similar narrative was pursued by Tony Blair when he became UK prime minister in 1997. SHA's Stepping Forward not only perpetuates such stigma, but serves a quadruple purpose of allowing rents to rise, reinforcing conditionality of access to public housing, creating sharp incentives for people to leave the system and thus, in theory, redistributing a scarce resource to those in greater need. Precisely the same policy and ideological motivations lie behind "Pay to Stay" in the UK's Housing and Planning Act 2016.[104]

---

[103] As in the UK, the US media has focused attention on the very rare exceptions.
[104] As part of a general retreat on key aspects of the Housing and Planning Act, in November 2016 the UK government announced that Pay to Stay would no longer be compulsory for council tenants, although it remains as a discretionary power for social landlords.

Housing and social justice campaigners in Seattle describe Stepping Forward as "a huge step back". They organised a series of large demonstrations demanding the policy be scrapped because it would be discriminatory, hitting immigrants, ethnic minorities and women disproportionately. They point out it ignored the reality that, no matter how much enforced "employment support" is provided, there are simply not enough jobs in Seattle paying wages that would allow public housing tenants to afford higher rents. Under additional pressure from the city's Mayor, in December 2014 SHA announced that it would "shelve" Stepping Forward until 2016 and possibly later.

Ideological gate keepers

Despite this victory, attempts to erect barriers to non-market housing continue on both sides of the Atlantic. The UK equivalents are found in a series of reforms by the 2010 Coalition and post-2015 Conservative governments, culminating in the Housing and Planning Act.

Disguised by its benign label, the 2011 Localism Act introduced important revisions to the founding principles of council housing, an intention made clear by the sentence "Previously almost anyone could apply to live in social housing, whether they need it or not".[105] The Act gave local authorities and housing associations far greater powers to restrict access to homes. These have been used by some to begin means-testing and remove thousands from waiting lists, while other organisations have begun to give priority to members of the armed services, a sign of the ideological dimension of the changes. The Act also allowed the introduction of time-limited tenancies, so non-market housing would increasingly be treated as "emergency" or temporary accommodation for a crisis period, after which tenants would be required to return to the "normality" of the market. In a direct similarity with Seattle's Stepping Forward

---

[105] DCLG (2011) *A Plain English Guide to the Localism Act* (p15), London, HMSO.

scheme, some housing associations have begun linking tenancies to compulsory employment support, with the same blindness to the scarcity of jobs that would enable working class people to afford market rents. The Act also further dismantles rights for the homeless. Previous legislation had already broken the entitlement of homeless people to be housed in the public sector. The Localism Act ensured that, in most cases, they would now be housed in the private rented sector and that this could be hundreds of miles from their original home. In parallel, the Coalition government began implementation of Affordable Rents, allowing subsidised social landlords to charge rents up to 80 per cent of the market level. The justification offered was that more funding would be available to build new homes. But the effect has been to create a multiple-tier system in which low income households are less likely to find a home they can afford, while achieving a Yesler Terrace-like demographic reordering of urban areas, favouring more affluent residents and commercially-oriented housing associations.

The 2016 Housing and Planning Act will accelerate these forces. Subject to further revisions in parliament and campaign pressure, the legislation is seen by many as a final push to kill off council housing and shift UK housing closer to the US model. Under Pay to Stay, the Act aims to make council and housing association tenants with an income above £31,000 a year (£40,000 in London) to pay a higher rent of 15 per cent for every £1 above the threshold. The Act will compel the sale of "higher value" council homes as they become empty, instead of renting them to the next people on the waiting list. The proceeds of these sales (or an equivalent levy) would be paid to private housing associations to off-set the subsidy for the Right to Buy that is being extended to housing associations tenants. The Act signals the phasing-out of secure lifetime tenancies for council tenants – a vital source of stability for working class communities – and their replacement with fixed-term tenancies like those in US public housing. Private property developers will be relieved of their obligations, however weakly interpreted and implemented, to build non-market homes for rent on new developments. Instead they will be encouraged to build Starter Homes for private sale (defined as "affordable housing") with government providing 20 per cent subsidies. The cumulative effect of these proposals would be to give more impetus to a revived Right to Buy system and hasten the privatisation of both council and housing association homes. As a result, the Chartered Institute of Housing has predicted a loss of 350,000 social rented homes by 2020. The Act would, if implemented, expose more housing to the mercy of the private property market, a long-held Tory ideological obsession.

A broad-based alliance of opposition has resisted the Act at every step. Founded in December 2015, "Axe the Housing Act" (originally called "Kill the Housing Bill") comprises tenants of all tenures, trade unions, sympathetic politicians, church leaders and housing activists. The campaign organised the biggest demonstration against government housing policy for a generation. Although the Housing and Planning Act was passed on 12th May 2016, it has been disintegrating ever since. Government has been forced to make concessions on some of its key provisions and as of spring 2017, the legislation is effectively stalled. However, it remains law and therefore a threat until it's repealed.

One of the most active campaigners against the Act, Janice Sweeney, describes herself as "a proud London council tenant". She explains why the issue was so important to her:

> Our rent was going to go up by 15 per cent because me and my husband earned over £40,000 jointly. I was horrified. We've always worked, doing worthwhile jobs in our community. I certainly didn't see myself as a 'high earner'. I got involved in the campaign and I've became aware of all the other bad things in the Act, like ending secure tenancies and reducing the overall amount of council housing. I was lucky to get a council home when I needed it. But I'm really worried about the situation for young people today and future generations. Until the Housing and Planning Act, I never paid attention to politics,

Axe the Housing Act demonstration, central London (18th June 2016).

but this campaign opened my eyes to a lot of very unfair, cruel legislation targeting working class people. But the campaign showed me people power does work and if you feel passionately about something and get organised you can change things.

Implicit within current US and UK housing policy are two shared and inter-linked ideological objectives. First is the attempt to destabilise and destroy any sense of entitlement that exists around non-market housing. This is most nakedly demonstrated in the UK by the Bedroom Tax, which leads to evicting tenants on benefits who are unable to either pay more for a "spare" bedroom in a home they may have occupied for decades or move to a smaller one. Second is the attempt to make all non-market tenants pay higher rents, based on the assumption that they could if only they'd try harder!

Re-Elect Kshama Sawant

One of the most vocal opponents of Stepping Forward in Seattle was socialist councillor Kshama Sawant. Ms Sawant was elected in 2013 challenging Seattle's social inequality and demanding the city be "affordable to all":

While construction cranes and luxury condos increasingly dominate our skyline, most of us face an affordable housing crisis. While our city and state are home to some of the world's wealthiest corporations, we face underfunded services and the most regressive tax system in the nation.[106]

Sawant's election flows from Seattle's rebellious past. As well as early co-operative settlements, in 1919 a five day general strike was the culmination of growing union militancy that included dock workers refusing to load weapons intended for the wars of intervention against revolutionary Russia. Seattle's ethnic diversity, typical of port cities, led to campaigns for civil rights from the late 1940s that anticipated those in the Deep South. The west-coast radicalism of the 1960s brought clashes over large-scale urban renewal projects and control over the planning system which contributed to the early development of alternative approaches to city life based on more humanistic values.[107] In 1999, Seattle was the setting for a highly significant moment in the history of political protest when trade unionists, radicals and an emerging contingent of environmentalists and new social movements joined together to protest against the presence of the World Trade Organisation and the global neoliberalism it represents.

On 8th June 2015, Kshama Sawant launched her campaign for re-election to the District 3 constituency[108] (which includes Yesler Terrace) at a public meeting attended by 800 people. Within her broad socialist manifesto – highlighting the extension of the $15 per hour minimum wage she was instrumental in getting Seattle to adopt – is a comprehensive list of housing reforms including rent control, building more public housing, a tenants' Bill of Rights, mortgage relief for low-income households and the establishment of a human right to housing for the homeless. Sawant's campaign

---

[106] http://www.kshamasawant.org/
[107] "Urban renewal threatens Seattle market", *New York Times*, 28th July 1971.
[108] Sawant comfortably won the election when it was held in November 2015.

has generated wide support and poses the critical question of the potential for a third party to emerge in America, with a detoxified housing policy at its heart.

Conclusions

The first president of the United States was a land speculator, but George Washington wasn't the last person to want to own a little piece of America or, in his case and that of John Malone, a lot of it! Native Americans believe that land cannot belong to people except to the extent that people belong to the land. But the housing crisis in Seattle exposes the multi-faceted struggle of working class Americans to belong in a place where belonging comes at an enormous price. Nickelsville and manufactured housing prove the capacity of people to find alternatives to the tyranny of the market and keep a toe-hold in their communities. The demolition of Seattle's first public housing exemplifies the hypocrisy and double-standards at the heart of US and UK housing policy. In some places "the problem" is high-rise, high-density modernism, but in Seattle it's low rise single family homes with gardens. In truth, the problem for corporate property interests is anything that impedes their ability to buy and sell our cities. The future of Yesler Terrace and Seattle as a whole now lies in the vagaries of the housing market.

5

Ups and downs in San Francisco

Introduction

Many aspects of Seattle's past, present and possible future are repeated writ large 800 miles down the coast in San Francisco. Here, too, a city is being turned inside out as long-established working class communities battle for survival amid a housing market on steroids. In a peninsula city, surrounded on three sides by water and with a dramatic topography featuring steep hills and an earthquake fault-line, the impact of unstable housing forces appear intensified. As in Seattle, the agency for this volatility is the influx of enormous wealth from the high tech industries whose highly paid staff work in near-by Silicon Valley but often choose to live in San Francisco. The richest five per cent of city residents have an average annual income of $423,171, substantially more than their equivalent in any other US city. San Francisco also has the highest number of "high net worth" individuals in America: 4,590 people have wealth of $30 million or more. But predictably, as the San Francisco rich have got richer, the poor have got poorer and more numerous. In 1990 66,000 house-holds in the city had annual income below $25,000; today that figure is 75,000. There has been a significant drop over the same period in the number of households earning between $25,000 and $75,000, from 130,000 to 95,000, suggesting the city's "middle class" is shrink-ing. Meanwhile, the number of households with income over $200,000 has risen from 13,000 to almost 40,000. This staggering income inequality is amplified by ethnicity. The city-wide median income in 2013 was $77,000. For white people it was $98,000, for Latinos $53,000, for African Americans $30,000.

This polarisation is reflected in San Francisco's bloated and volatile housing market. The median price of a single family home has risen by 61 per cent since 2011. Rents have risen by 52 per cent since 2000 and by 18 per cent between 2014 and 2015. Overall, house prices in the Bay Area boomed by 75 per cent between 2000 and 2006 and then bust, falling by 45 per cent between the 2007 crash and 2009, since when the speculative bubble has started to steadily reflate.

Welcome Home

An emerging actor in San Francisco's housing crisis is Airbnb. The giant "social capitalist" corporation worth $20 billion has an estimated 5,000 listings in the city where it was created. Housing campaigners claim this is reducing the availability of permanent homes for rent and therefore Airbnb – slogan "welcome home" – has become an agent of displacement and a legitimate political target. On 9th June 2015, hundreds of San Franciscans crammed into the city's ornate council chamber for a meeting of their elected officials, the Board of Supervisors. On the agenda were measures aimed at controlling the activities of Airbnb by restricting the number of nights "hosts" could offer a year and introducing a system of regulation. Demonstrators held signs reading "Tenants not Tourists!" and "Homes not Hotels!" Airbnb hosts pointed to their constitutional rights. The issue provokes strong passions and is a fascinating insight into both the complexity of the housing crisis and America's response to it.

The move to curtail Airbnb was introduced by a local politician, David Campos. He represents the Mission district, one of the epicentres of San Francisco's housing rift, where, he claims, 2,000 potential rental homes are taken off the market by Airbnb. Campos argues that high yields, low regulation and flexibility create a huge incentive for property owners to convert from being private landlords to Airbnb hosts. In this process, not only are potential tenants denied homes, but existing tenants, particularly those covered by rent control, are being displaced. Campos and his supporters give numerous examples of opportunist and sometimes coerced evictions by landlords hoping to cash in on the Airbnb bubble. They argue that, far from the folksy, personal image, some hosts are operating on an institutional scale, with multiple buildings devoted to short-term lets, leading to what Campos describes as the "hotelisation and privatisation" of entire neighbourhoods. As well as generating levels of disturbance that would not otherwise be associated with residential areas, Airbnb's opponents argue that its model of transience undermines community stability and identity. Moreover, this activity takes place without any of the supervision that would accompany the orthodox hospitality industry, including the allegation that Airbnb hosts have no real idea who is staying in their homes, making them a potential security risk, may not comply with fire safety standards and don't always pay tax. To combat these abuses, Campos wanted the City Council to limit hosts to 60 Airbnb nights a year and introduce a system of registration and monitoring.

On the other side of the argument are sentiments that connect both with deep-rooted American beliefs and attitudes to the 21st century city. In a recurring theme of the US housing crisis, Airbnb hosts invoke their fundamental freedom to do as they like with their property. However, the debate is more nuanced than this. Some hosts claim that, without the supplementary income from Airbnb, they themselves would be priced out of the city. They also point to the intrinsic informality of Airbnb as a way of promoting cultural diversity, mutual understanding and trust, based on a fluidity in tune with the "networked" city and global economy. This flexibility is threatened by a system of external bureaucratic administration that again raises totemic issues about the extent of government involvement in the lives and homes of American citizens.

The decision of the San Francisco Board of Supervisors on 9th June 2015 was not to make a decision! It was apparent that both Airbnb and hotel chains wanting to trim a source of competition had been lobbying heavily and that large-scale commercial and political interests were at stake. After anti-Airbnb protesters had been ejected for making too much noise, the conclusion was that a further period of deliberation was needed. However, the Airbnb issue is not going away and is playing out in other American (and European) cities where it is a lightning rod for the conflicts of class and privilege that underscore the housing crisis.[109]

---

[109] The San Francisco Board of Supervisors did subsequently agree limits on Airbnb activities, as politicians have in other cities, but these were challenged in the courts by the company. "San Francisco proposes 60-day hard cap on Airbnb rentals", *San Francisco Examiner*, 13th October 2016.

The Ellis Act and rent control

Similar debates and political compromises surround regulation of the private rented sector in San Francisco. Tenants' demands for protection from rent rises and eviction are countered by landlords claiming "property rights" and pointing to perceived dangers of inhibiting the free market. As in New York City, one of the anomalies of San Francisco's housing situation is the intended countervailing force of the Ellis Act, a system of legislative control over private renting. The Act covers the state of California and seeks to limit the circumstances under which landlords can withdraw property from the rental market. It allows them to do so only by meeting certain criteria designed to stop long-term tenants being frivolously evicted. To comply with the Act, landlords must demonstrate they are "going out of business" by completely emptying their property of existing tenants thus, supposedly, preventing individual households from being singled out or victimised, while enshrining the sacrosanct property rights of the owner. However, Ellis assumes a parity of power between landlords and tenants in San Francisco's over-heated housing market. With huge financial incentives for "flipping" property, the measures intended to protect tenants are having the opposite effect. A mapping project by a housing justice campaign records 4,014 San Francisco families forced out of their homes since 1997 by owners 'Ellising' their properties in order to convert them to more lucrative private condominiums or Airbnb use.

San Francisco also has a system of rent control that may be having similarly mixed results. Most private tenants in the city are covered by the restriction on rent rises, currently pegged at 1.9 per cent per annum and administered by a Rent Board. A similar system existed in the UK prior to the abolition of "Fair Rents" in the early 1980s and the introduction of Assured Shorthold Tenancies in 1989. There are a number of loopholes in the San Francisco system. Buildings constructed after 1979 are exempted, so although the city has a prized stock of Victorian and early 20th century homes, there is a massive fall-off of rent control for post-1980 buildings. None of the 8,000 new apartments due to be built between 2015 and 2017 nor the 15,000 in the development pipeline are covered, a clear sign of the shape of things to come. The Rent Board process is largely initiated by tenants, with no compulsory registration of landlords so, as with the Ellis Act, the extent of protection relies upon the naïve view that the relationship between landlords and tenants is essentially one of equals.

This is particularly unrealistic alongside San Francisco's speculative property frenzy where fortunes are being made and the demand for decent housing far exceeds supply. Four statistics indicate the limitations of rent control and regulation for protecting private tenants in the context of a chronically unbalanced housing system. Alleged wrongful evictions in San Francisco rose by 19 per cent in 2014 and total evictions by six per cent; average rents in the city have risen by 57 per cent since 2010 and the current median rent is $3,200 per month, the highest in the US. At a time when demands for greater regulation of the UK's private rented sector are growing, the San Francisco experience is a reminder that such controls can be very porous.

Mission creep

The Mission District is the epitome of the dramatic social, economic and cultural colonisation often described as gentrification. Named after the Mission San Francisco de Asis on Dolores Street (built in 1776, the same year another part of America was declaring independence[110]), the area is still home to a large Spanish-speaking, working class community. But the tides of change are captured (in what is almost a checklist for the 21st century gentrification aesthetic) by Airbnb:

> The Mission District's multifarious corridors comprise an invitingly seedy melting pot of cultures, cuisines, and cool kids. Dusty produce

---

[110] At this time, California and most of what we now know as south-western USA was part of Mexico.

bins line the sidewalks in front of colourful Latino markets, and the aroma of fresh roasted coffee beans emanates from first-class cafes along this diverse neighborhood's main streets. Whether you're looking for upscale restaurants, lowbrow dive bars, the best taquerias,[111] or simply delicious street food, the Mission delivers.[112]

The Mission is one of the areas of choice for cash-rich, high-tech executives. Anecdotal evidence reports homes in the Mission being bought, in cash, for substantially more than the asking price, which average one million dollars. The *New York Times* offers a different description of the area:

> The local colour is still here: splashy murals, many with political themes, provide open-air art on numerous buildings. But the housing prices have risen well beyond the reach of the average artist: studio apartments in the Mission are listed on Zillow, the real estate site, for $2,700 a month and one-bedroom for $3,800. When a family in a rent-controlled apartment leaves or is forced out, the rent is jacked up to market rate, apartments become condominiums or are advertised by the landlord on Airbnb as a good place for short-term visits.[113]

Academics at the Universities of Berkeley and UCLA have examined the complex interplay of factors driving neighbourhood transformation in San Francisco and the adjoining Bay Area. By looking at issues including housing costs, the presence of desirable period homes, investment in public transport and changes in the jobs market, the researchers identify "risk factors" contributing to displacement and gentrification (terms they stress are not interchangeable). They conclude that the Mission is in a state of "advanced gentrification" characterised by the loss of affordable homes and a demographic shift with fewer residents from low or medium income households. Although the Mission has been more

---

[111] A type of Mexican restaurant.
[112] Airbnb website.
[113] "Gentrification spreads an upheaval in San Francisco's Mission district", *New York Times*, 22nd May 2015.

affected by these changes than any other part of the city, the research finds that other parts of San Francisco are also "at risk".[114]

Priced out and buy outs

Marilyn Duran was born and raised in the Mission, where she lives with her mum (who came to the US from Nicaragua) and brother. From the age of 13, Marilyn got involved in '¡PODER!', a grassroots housing and environmental justice campaign whose name translates to 'Power' in Spanish. In one of the few remaining cheap restaurants on Valencia Street, Marilyn reflects on the changes in her neighbourhood:

> It's mostly white, young, high-income people who work in the tech industry who are moving in. People on low and middle incomes, that would probably be fine in most other cities, are really struggling to make it in San Francisco. Some are being evicted; others are leaving because they've been offered $5,000 per person to quit so the owners can flip their home. The landlord thinks "I have a family paying $1,200 for a two bedroom when I can raise that to $4,000 or more by renting to a different family who aren't covered by rent control". My family received that offer, but we ignored it.

> It's not just housing. The Mission used to have lots more mom and pop stores and bodegas. Some have survived, but many have been priced out. My family has an income of about $50,000 between three adults. But we'd need at least twice that to live in the Mission if we didn't have a controlled rent.

The "buy outs" Marilyn refers to illustrate the daily reality for thousands of Mission residents and the enormous profits at stake for landlords and developers. Marilyn's family received a letter from their landlord quoting the Ellis Act and offering them $15,000 to move out of the home they've lived in for 17 years. The other family

---

[114] See http://www.urbandisplacement.org/

San Francisco mural.

living in the building eventually accepted the offer and was dispersed around the Bay Area. One of the daughters moved to San Carlos, 20 miles south-east of San Francisco, where housing is still expensive but rents are about half the San Francisco level. An approximate UK comparison having similar consequences is a rapidly transforming area just north of the commercial City of London, ridiculously branded Silicon Roundabout. Until ten years ago, this was a predominantly working class neighbourhood; it has become a high-tech "hub" centred on Old Street roundabout with attendant high-end apartments, bars and restaurants. There are some people making a lot of money, but still significant pockets of deprivation and growing pressure for low- and medium-income people to move to places with cheaper housing. The average monthly rent for a two-bedroom home is £3,230 per month. Twenty miles to the south-east is the town of Dartford in Kent where the equivalent rent is £979.

The Mission is noted for its Mexican-inspired street art. Colourful murals adorn walls around the area, many with strong political messages in which housing and gentrification feature prominently. One is titled *Narratives of Displacement*. It records 12,000 "no fault" evictions and 33,000 people displaced in San Francisco since 1997 and "the latest tech BOOM!" Sitting above the images of some of those unable to stay in the city are a young, obviously affluent couple under a heading "Welcome to San Francisco – cleaner, whiter, brighter".

Fight back

Marilyn's family are resisting attempts to displace them, although their landlord is now trying to use "just cause" to evict by making trumped-up allegations of breeches of tenancy conditions, similar to some of those heard in the Chicago eviction court. As pressure increases on the remaining working class Latino community of the Mission, it is fighting harder to stay put by getting involved in the kind of campaigns that have long been a part of San Francisco's housing and political history.

To the north of the Mission is the Ping Yuen ("tranquil garden") public housing development. Built in response to campaigns by the Chinese community for more affordable homes, it opened in 1951 at a ceremony attended by 5,000 people. Like Yesler Terrace in Seattle, Ping Yuen defies the stereotype of identical US public housing, incorporating distinctive Oriental design features. However, what Ping Yuen tenants did have in common with those in other places was an institutional landlord with an impervious, bureaucratic mentality. Signs that the San Francisco Housing Authority (SFHA) was not maintaining the early promise of the city's public housing led to the formation in 1966 of the Ping Yuen Residents Improvements Association (PYRIA). In October 1978, 200 tenants organised a rent strike to protest against their housing conditions and incidents of appalling violence seemingly ignored by the authorities. For the next three and a half months, PYRIA members went door-to-door to collect the rent, paying it into an escrow account pending resolution of the dispute, which continued even after SFHA had issued eviction notices. PYRIA made contact with other public housing tenant organisations – of all ethnicities – and received messages of solidarity that endured as stronger community links after the rent strike's victorious conclusion. In January 1979, SFHA committed to a range of repairs and security improvements. The rent strike resumed when they failed to carry them out. As Amy Howard[115] argues, Ping Yuen and similar examples of working class organisation around housing are a "clarion call for 21st century public housing that is more than shelter".

Just south of the Mission is Bayview-Hunters Point. The area has been the centre of the city's African-American community since the migration from the South that brought thousands to work in the nearby navy shipyards in the 1930s and 1940s. The government built wartime barrack-like accommodation for shipyard workers and their families that was originally segregated. But black and white people formed united tenant campaigns demanding better conditions, particularly after the war when the homes were transferred to SFHA. However, in a recurring pattern, this glimpse of an ethnically integrated community with public housing at its heart was short lived. In 1954 the shipyard started mass redundancies and many white families moved away. Poor African-American families were left behind with few jobs, a deteriorating, contaminated environment and institutional racism. In 1966 a young, unarmed black man, Matthew Johnson, was shot in the back and killed by a white policeman sparking the Hunters Point Rebellion. In the same period a group of local women resolved to fight back against the marginalisation and brutalisation of their community. They organised pickets of shops with discriminatory practices, and a rent strike against the housing authority's neglect. The Bayview-Hunters Point

---

[115] A L Howard (2014) *More Than Shelter: Activism and community in San Francisco public housing*, Minneapolis, University of Minnesota Press.

Housing Committee fought for and won significant funding in the 1970s that led to the building of new homes, employment projects and community facilities. But the vicious cycle of under-investment and decline again gripped the area, exacerbated by the crack epidemic of the 1980s and 1990s. Bayview-Hunters Point missed out in San Francisco's uneven influx of affluence. The predictable official response was the announcement in 2011 that local public housing would be included in HUD's Choice Neighbourhoods programme. Throughout its chequered past, Bayview-Hunters Point has remained relatively affordable, but large-scale redevelopment fuelled by San Francisco's high octane housing market now threatens displacement and gentrification.

Like his counterparts in Boston, New York and Chicago, the Mayor of San Francisco knows the city's housing crisis requires an urgent political response. Ed Lee established his political reputation as a radical lawyer advising the Ping Yuen rent strikers, but is now more commonly known for his lobbying links to high-tech industries. In September 2015, Lee announced that making San Francisco affordable again was his "No.1" priority, despite the fact that the proportion of non-market homes has continued to fall under his administration. Lee's policies rely on a stale cocktail of tinkering with targets without confronting the fundamental issue of speculative development feeding on the city's grotesque income inequality. Lee's reluctance to challenge big business interests means he has opposed curbs on Airbnb and demands for a moratorium on new development in the Mission. Like other establishment politicians in the US and UK, Mayor Lee has a slavish belief that private developers are the answer to the problem, not the cause.

As Marilyn Duran testifies, the crumbs of affordable housing falling from the speculators' table are simply inadequate and constitute "a lottery". Despite Mayor Lee's reassurances, Marilyn doesn't expect to be in the Mission in five years' time. She says "We'll have to move east and we'll probably be in Nevada or Arizona before we

Window poster, San Francisco.

find housing we can afford. There are entire families pitching tents under freeways. It's sickening".

Eviction resistance

At 6am on 9th June 2015, a crowd began to gather in the drizzly rain outside a home at 812 Guerrero Street in the Mission District. This home was bought for $1.4 million in 2012 by a senior Google executive. By 7am about 70 people had formed a blockade to prevent the planned eviction of a tenant under the Ellis Act. The frequency of evictions in San Francisco has made campaigners well practiced in resistance. Using social media networks, different activist groups combine to mount lively, well organised, assertive demonstrations complete with loud-speakers and musical instruments. Early in the morning, in a relatively quiet residential area, this could attract a negative response, but there is something quintessentially American about the spirit and energy of US housing campaigners. They are unapologetic, articulate, media savvy and seek to appeal to a deep-rooted sense of social justice and solidarity. Some of this was captured in a speech on the steps of the Guerrero Street building by one of the tenants threatened with eviction, Evan Wolkenstein:

> A lot of people think that houses and apartments are commodities, places you can buy and sell. In a way that's true and we see it all the time in San Francisco. But there's another way of thinking about it – in terms of justice and power. There are people with endless resources buying up the homes of people with none and because of the economic situation in this city, people can't find other homes. In San Francisco, to be displaced from your home is to be displaced from the city: a one-way ticket to somewhere else. It's devastating, but there are some people who are more vulnerable than others, maybe because English is a second language, or they're immigrants who don't know their rights, or are sick or ageing and so their ability to fight back is compromised. I joined this cause to protect my home, but I also felt a responsibility to fight for others, like Becky. She has a disability that makes it difficult for her to keep up with the legal paperwork. She doesn't have the resources to find a new place to live. She's scared and alone. She needs her home, but the reality is that if she loses it, Becky will probably end up on the streets.'

Becky was the woman the Sheriff was due to evict that day. She had lived at 812 Guerrero Street for 25 years and suffered from

Eviction Resistance, Guerrero Street, San Francisco.

mental ill-health. After several hours of chanting and waving of banners reading "This is a community, not a Monopoly board" and "El barrio estácontigo" (The neighbourhood is with you) it appeared the eviction wasn't going to happen that day. It was soon to be thrown into unexpected abeyance when, less than a month later, the Google executive landlord died an untimely death. Profiteering, evictions and displacement did not die with him.

Old and New Sacramento

A two-hour, 90-mile train ride north-east from San Francisco, is 'Old' Sacramento. Historic buildings are preserved that enshrine the myths and reality of the Wild West in what could be a Western film-set. Following Spanish and Mexican colonisation and the dispossession of the Nisenan and Miwok Native Americans, in 1848 Sacramento became a centre for the California Gold Rush. Today it's the state capital of California, the seat of political power. While the housing situation in San Francisco is grossly distended, the ramifications ripple out into the state that was the most severely affected by subprime and its consequences. When the housing market crashed in 2007-08, nearly taking global capitalism with it, 785,000 Californian families lost their homes. Sacramento had the fifth highest number of foreclosures in the US at an estimated cost to the local economy of $7.5 billion.

Subprime and the credit crunch have been exhaustively analysed, but often with a sense that this was a massive natural disaster: unforeseeable, uncontrollable and unlikely to recur in the near future. The experience of Sacramento demonstrates the opposite. The bubble that eventually burst began inflating in the 1990s and expanded dramatically in the 2000s through a lethal combination of available land (much of it formerly agricultural), available finance (much of it in the form of credit) and an avaricious property development industry operating on a gargantuan scale. Alyssa Katz[116] has meticulously chronicled how the Sacramento area was transformed as it became the new frontier of speculative house building. Between 1996 and 2006, 140,000 new homes were built and sold in and around the city, particularly in some of its outer suburbs such as Lincoln (30 miles north), which was the fastest-growing settlement in the US between 2000 and 2010, growing by 282 per cent! As Katz notes, a large number of the new residents were "real estate refugees" from the Bay Area, while others were drawn to the "exurbs" by the promise of a lifestyle detached from the anxieties – actual or perceived – of city life. This was a re-enactment of a defining American impulse, but on a greater scale even than the post-

---

[116] Katz A (2009) *Our Lot: How real estate came to own us*, New York, Bloomsbury.

war urban exodus exploited by the Levitts (p42). The relatively modest homes they built on Long Island were dwarfed by the iden-tikit McMansions, ironically sold as an expression of individuality and typically over 3,000 square feet in size.[117] Alyssa Katz summarises the wider implications:

> And so at a time of spiking oil prices, global warming, infernal traffic and ever-lengthening commute times, homebuyers voted with their wheels...In less than 30 years, as a nation we've more than doubled the amount of space we live in and therefore have to heat, cool and power – space that accounts for as much greenhouse gas production as all the cars, trucks and buses in America. In the process we also doubled the number of miles we collectively drive every year, to about three trillion. While the United States was heading into war for oil in Iraq, the nation's homebuilders were serving a feast of petroleum consumption and carbon gluttony.

The environmental damage of laissez faire housing is stark in California, which was in the throes of a serious drought in 2015 and where the supply and equitable distribution of water is a growing anxiety. As in the UK, the heedless search for maximum profit drives developers to build in places and with methods and materials that ignore the laws of nature, as well as economics. Although California is often very dry, Old Sacramento offers a reminder that this is not always the case. The original city had to be raised a level because it was constantly flooded by the Sacramento River, but like their UK counterparts, developers continue to build new homes on the flood plain.

Discriminatory lending and foreclosures

One injustice of the subprime meltdown was how it disproportion-ately affected African-Americans and other ethnic minorities. After

---

[117] The average US house is approximately 2,000 feet square, over twice the size of the UK's homes which are among the smallest in the developed world.

decades in which many had been denied access to mortgages, partly as a mechanism for excluding them from certain areas after explicit segregation became unlawful – a practice known as "redlining" – at the turn of the 21st century non-white Americans became the prime targets for predatory and fraudulent lending. Households already earning significantly below average median income were offered a chance to buy homes. Lenders didn't care that loans soon became unaffordable. They were merely components of exotic mortgage "products" traded on global markets, generating fortunes in fees and commissions. In 2006, half of all home loans in predominantly non-white neighbourhoods of Sacramento were subprime, a pattern replicated in other Californian cities. When the scheme collapsed, the effect on black and minority ethnic communities was devastating. According to the California Reinvestment Coalition:

> The foreclosure crisis has created one of the greatest losses of personal and neighbourhood wealth in US history. One estimate places the total loss of wealth among African-American households at between $72 billion and $93 billion...[118]

More likely to be sold subprime mortgages, after the crash non-white Americans were less likely to receive government help to bail them out and more likely to have their homes repossessed following foreclosure. In total, nine million Americans lost their homes and African-Americans and Latinos were three times more likely to fall victim. Research by Cornell University in 2015 found that widespread abandonment "fuelled racial segregation" as white households previously living in mixed neighbourhoods moved out and were replaced by non-whites taking advantage of cheaper housing.

The abuses of subprime lending have often been portrayed as the acts of unscrupulous, unregulated rogue lenders. In fact a substan-

---

[118] 'From Foreclosure to Re-Redlining: How America's largest financial institutions devastated California communities', California Reinvestment Coalition, February 2010.

tial proportion of high-risk mortgages were issued by big corporate banks which were particularly active in non-white neighbourhoods. The consequences, researchers at Cornell University say, "could alter the complexion of American cities for a generation or more".[119]

Housing bubble two

The US in general and Sacramento in particular have yet to recover from subprime. The crisis dumped thousands of devalued homes on to the market, many then hoovered up and re-sold by the same banks who issued the failing mortgages! And yet, there are now warnings of another housing bubble created by rising prices, cheap borrowing and market manipulation. In Sacramento, cash-rich speculative investors are pushing individual buyers out of the way and accumulating portfolios which they hoard, flip or rent, all in the hope that prices will continue to rise. The 2015 feature film *99 Homes* (directed by Ramin Bahrani) graphically captures the dehumanising process. If they're "lucky", those squeezed out of the market are consigned to long-term, expensive renting. If they're unlucky, they end up homeless. But there's a massive looming problem facing the US housing casino. In Sacramento and across the nation, house prices are outstripping wages by an average of 13 per cent, a dislocation that will ultimately lead to prices falling and precipitate another crash before the tremors of the last one have passed.

The Resolution Foundation has found a very similar pattern in the UK, where house prices rose five times faster than wages between 2011 and 2016, and comments:

> Runaway house prices have had a clear feed through to living standards in recent years. Most obviously it has priced people out of homeownership, pushing significant numbers into the private rental market.

---

[119] Hall M, Crowder K and Spring A *Neighbourhood Foreclosures, Racial/Ethnic Transitions and Residential Segregation* in American Sociological Review, Vol. 80 issue 3, April 2015.

But rampant house price inflation isn't just a problem for wannabe home-owners. It has increased the stock of mortgage debt, and fuelled demand for renting that is driving up costs there too. Ultimately we all pay for house price inflation by spending a greater share of our incomes on housing.

The solution to this housing crisis isn't easy – especially in London. It will require radical action to both boost the supply of housing for all tenure types, and improve conditions and security in the UK's private rental sector.[120]

It's a wonderful life

At the heart of subprime, foreclosure, repossession, homelessness and every other aspect of the endemic crisis resulting from neoliberal housing policy is the deification of home ownership. The US economy is now heavily dependent on and skewed towards maintaining the financial and moral superiority of owning your own home, or as it is sometimes more accurately referred to "renting from the bank". At one level, home ownership is a perfectly understandable and reasonable personal desire, at another it is a grand social illusion. Enslavement to the ideology of housing as an expression of identity and worth should be set alongside the loss of $2.7 trillion in US housing wealth as a result of subprime and foreclosure, to say nothing of the manifold social costs.

Few things capture the contradictory essence of America's relationship to homeownership like the film *It's a Wonderful Life*. When there's a run on his small independent bank, George Bailey (James Stewart) makes an impassioned plea to its small-town investors to recognise the benefits of mutual lending as a model for allowing working class people to buy their home and achieve independence from corporate capitalists like Henry F Potter (Lionel Barrymore):

---

[120] *Living Standards 2016: The experience of low to middle income households in downturn and recovery*, The Resolution Foundation, February, 2016.

...he [Potter] wants to keep you in his slums and paying the kind of rent he decides. Joe, you had one of those Potter houses. Have you forgotten what he charged you for that broken-down shack? Ed, you remember last year when things weren't going so well and you couldn't make your payments: well you didn't lose your home. Do you think Potter would have let you keep it? We've got to stick together and have faith in each other.

Although a romanticised eulogy for a by-gone age, some of the film's key themes still resonate. But the hope of home-ownership as an escape from slumlords and corporate loan-sharks now has a mocking quality for millions of Americans.

An Englishman's home...

A very similar, if smaller scale, ideological construct underpins housing policy in the UK, where owning a home has come to embody powerful meanings of personal fulfilment, social respectability, status and potential failure. The following homily comes from a marketing campaign for a property company website (*primelocation.com*). Alongside scenes of idealised domesticity (dogs, gleaming kitchens, log fires) a lilting commentary intones:

Your dream home paid for with graft, sweat and sacrifice. This is your prize for building up a business one customer at a time. This is your trophy for juggling conference calls while toddlers shriek and teenagers strop... This is your temple of tranquillity...this is your reward – and deservedly so.

Since 2008 the UK government has been forced to confront the failure of the home ownership orthodoxy, not least with enormous cash bailouts to the housing market and financial system. For the first time in almost a century, home ownership is falling. Many young people have given up on the idea of buying a home, deepening the inter-generational wealth divide to which housing policy is a major contributor. US and UK governments are now faced with a gap between their attempts to re-establish the economic and ideological supremacy of owner-occupation, and the impossibility for many of their electorate of turning the "dream of home ownership" into reality.

American tragedy

Charlotte Delgado has lived in Sacramento for 30 years, but in 2015 found that she didn't have a home there. Charlotte moved to her rented apartment in the city centre in 1985. Soon after, she became a tenant activist when she led a successful battle to keep rents affordable for herself and her fellow low-income neighbours. This was a life-changing moment for Charlotte because it led her to the National Alliance of HUD Tenants (NAHT), a national, tenant-led organisation that campaigns to preserve and protect affordable housing, particularly in the private rented sector. Charlotte has been a NAHT Board member ever since and was the organisation's national chairperson for several years until her own housing situation destabilised her life.

When the latest speculative property boom hit Sacramento, Charlotte's building was "flipped" three times in three years, each time increasing a sense of threat and vulnerability. Charlotte was a marked woman because the owners knew her reputation and that she would organise to resist any attempt to hike rents or evict low income tenants. They made Charlotte various offers – including outright bribes – in the hope she'd leave quietly. She refused. In early May 2015, Charlotte received an eviction order based on spurious grounds relating to the behaviour of her younger son who is chronically ill and mentally unstable. One day Charlotte returned home from visiting a sick neighbour she cared for to find the building manager and the sheriff changing the locks. She had to demand the return of her walking frame and purse before she was told to leave the building. At the age of 79, Charlotte was homeless and alone. She says she spent the rest of the day in a daze, walking around the city until she couldn't walk any more. This wouldn't attract attention in Sacramento because there are thousands of people in a similar plight. The local homeless encampment has elected its own Mayor and there's a dedicated school for homeless children. Charlotte had spent years volunteering at a shelter, but never imagined she'd need its help. She recalled that another thing she'd never considered was where homeless women go to the toilet when, like her, they (literally) have no place to go.

Fortunately, at least some of Charlotte's contribution to society was repaid and she was offered emergency shelter so she didn't have to sleep on the street. She was then provided with temporary accommodation by a Catholic charity, while she tried to find a permanent home. Although she was now in a comfortable, caring environment, the hostel was in the suburbs, a one hour train and bus ride from the neighbourhood she knows. It was as though Charlotte had been banished from the city for daring to challenge the property barons. She tried to get help from the public housing authority, but despite her age and physical frailty, they weren't interested. Instead Charlotte had to hope that her housing voucher would be honoured by a new private landlord, but this was in some doubt because technically, Charlotte had been evicted for breaching her tenancy conditions. In early August, after three months of dislocated limbo, Charlotte found an apartment in a complex for older people, but her uncertainty was not over yet. A month later, the housing authority, which administers the voucher system, had not released the funding to pay the landlord. So Charlotte had a bed and a roof over her head, but her furniture was still in storage because she wanted to be certain that she wasn't going to be made homeless again.

In the context of a flimsy, porous social welfare system, Charlotte has been relatively fortunate to be rehoused. Others, like Charlotte's older son, are not so lucky. After serving in the US Army, he worked as a gardener for the city for 25 years and had been living with his mum and acting as her carer before her eviction. He ended up on the streets, along with his younger brother, who Charlotte thinks

Charlotte Delgado.

may have stomach cancer because he keeps vomiting blood. Referring to another aspect of America's relentless war on the poor, Charlotte relates an occasion when she went to the chemist with her
younger son and asked how many of the 11 drugs he needed she
could afford with the $55 she had in her purse. The answer was
"none". The cheapest prescription was $110.

American hero

It's one thing to witness and try to describe the experience of those affected by America's housing crisis, another when one of its victims is a personal friend. I've known Charlotte Delgado for about ten years and she's one of the most remarkable people I've ever met. She's devoted much of her life to helping others, particularly campaigning with NAHT for tenants' rights and decent homes for all. But Charlotte's story is about much more than housing. She defied potential racist prejudice by marrying a Mexican, became a fluent Spanish speaker, spent many years working in the hotel industry, fostered and adopted abandoned children, is an active church member, a cancer survivor, but still chain-smokes the cigarettes she calls "coffin nails". Charlotte's politics aren't formulated through theory or party affiliation, but an innate sense of social justice and class solidarity that is distinctively American. This is also reflected in her patriotism which, most remarkably, is undimmed by the loss of three (yes, three) sons in the Vietnam War. But as she approaches her 80s, Charlotte isn't bitter or self-pitying, just angry with a system that destroys lives for profit. Despite her age and some health problems, Charlotte was still fighting for the homes of others when she lost her own. She's already told NAHT that once she's settled in her new home she'll organise a tenants association![121]

The hardest thing for Charlotte in telling me her story (and for me listening to it) is that she feels ashamed. Like other activists I've known, Charlotte is better at fighting for others than herself. Given all she's done to help other people and the affection she's held in, it's possible Charlotte could have avoided the situation she found herself in when she lost her home, but not certain. A key feature of American society in general and its housing crisis in particular, is its brutality. The fact that Charlotte Delgado is elderly, disabled, poor and has made huge contributions to and sacrifices for her

---

[121] Since 2015, Charlotte's housing situation has stabilised. She's been able to settle in a new apartment in central Sacramento, sharing with her older son.

country, including paying taxes for 65 years, matters not a jot. When the forces of corporate finance, property developers and their political lackies want to make money, it seems nothing else matters. If California was a country, it would be the seventh wealthiest on earth. Who should be ashamed?

Conclusions

For centuries, people came to California from all over the world in the hope of finding gold. When Steinbeck's Joad family left Oklahoma, California was their destination of hope. Hollywood has projected a glamorous image of the state around the world and today a new seam of riches is mined by microchip. But all that glitters is not gold. When the Joads crossed the Colorado River, their struggles had only just begun: to establish a home for themselves in a community of the dispossessed. Around Sacramento's Cesar Chavez Plaza, named in honour of a union leader and civil rights activist, in 2015 "dumpster diving" is a common sight – peoples' heads buried in rubbish bins as they scavenge for food. California is a place where a 79 year-old woman can be made homeless and have to rely on charity to save her from joining her two sons – one of them chronically sick – sleeping on the streets. In California, housing has become the arbiter of success and failure: the source of fortunes for a few and constant struggle for many. San Francisco provides the ultimate example of how the commodification of shelter, sponsored by growth junkies and boom and bust deniers, contains the seeds of its own destruction. The 1990s "dot com" bonanza saw a 56 per cent increase in house prices until the crash of 2000 brought thousands of job losses and a deep property market slump. Seven years later, the promise of home ownership for all was incinerated in the bonfire of the subprime vanities, leading to the Great Recession from which neither the US nor UK working class have yet recovered, unlike the bankers who created it. Another seven years on and there are warnings that Housing Bubble Two might be about to burst in California, with inevitable

Dumpster diving in Sacramento.

consequences beyond the state. The damage, causes and potential solutions are summed up by Charlotte Delgado:

> The government is trying to balance the budget on the backs of the poor and poorest – women, veterans and the disabled. They're cutting programmes for affordable housing, but there are no cuts in the military budget. I'm a mother of seven veterans, including three who are over on the wall.[122] Our veterans need to be looked after by bringing them home. We need to make sure that big corporations like Apple and Bank of America pay their fair share of taxes. I pay mine. We're here because the government needs to see the faces of the people their cuts affect. We need a government that recognises decent housing as a basic human right. (Speaking at NAHT conference, Washington DC, June 2014.)

---

[122] A reference to the Vietnam War Memorial in Washington DC.

6

New Orleans: Neoliberalism in the raw

Introduction

The housing crisis and America's urban malaise rarely penetrate the national consciousness. Understandably, given the size of the country, its federal structure and distinctive regional characteristics, the news media and political machinery tends to focus at city, or at most, at state level. Since 29th August 2005, the exception has been New Orleans. The catastrophic events that followed Hurricane Katrina drew attention to a spectrum of issues that are common to many other US (and UK) cities, but were thrown into dramatic relief in the "Crescent City". Access to a decent, secure, affordable home; homelessness; the privatisation of public housing; urban dispossession; displacement and gentrification; discriminatory and racist urban policy; criminalisation of the poor; environmental neglect; history, cultural memory and identity; rapacious property development; inequality; abuses of political and corporate power. All are subjects of concern throughout the US. But with the destructive drama of natural disaster, New Orleans has become a symbol for the malevolence of a housing model based on private profit.

To all of these factors must be added the special quality of New Orleans itself, an enigmatic city where a mixture of cultures struggles with a traumatised past amidst architectural splendour, de facto segregation and institutionalised hedonism (in the form of the tourist and "conferencing" industry), all alongside one of the most impoverished urban populations in the US. The events of 2005 could have happened in many other places in America, but it's unlikely they would have had the same kaleidoscopic impact as in New Orleans. Dylan Thomas once described his home town of Swansea as "ugly lovely". A similar label (and also "very hot and humid") could fit New Orleans. Katrina threw up a host of deeply troubling issues that have far wider implications for US society. Politicians, property developers, "non-profits" and others gathered around the damaged city and embarked on a project to rebuild it along neoliberal lines. Amid chaos, death and destruction, State-sponsored coercion and brutality were used to subdue an already

Charles Smith, Lower 9th Ward.

traumatised population in an attempt to control the people and institutions allowed to come back. Access to housing was used as a mechanism for social cleansing. How did they get away with it?

The Lower Ninth

On 13th June 2015, Charles Smith was sitting on the dilapidated porch of his family home on North Galvez Street. He had electricity, but no running water and visited neighbours to wash. His single-storey wooden house was held together with plywood, the roof barely intact and the surrounding area overgrown and scattered with debris. The roads were rutted, fallen telephone wires mingled with overhanging trees. Many of the other homes around Charles' were apparently damaged beyond repair and abandoned. This was the Lower Ninth Ward ten years after Katrina.

In yet another example of the incorrigible optimism of many Americans, Charles was looking forward to the day when the family's insurance payment finally arrived and he could afford to repair his home. He echoed a spirit that drove the development of the Lower Ninth, where generations of African-American families, many of them from rural backgrounds, had bought cheap land outside the city centre and built their own homes, which they owned in higher proportions than other New Orleanians.

After Katrina, the two-mile square district downriver from downtown, bordered on three sides by water, became emblematic of the city's misery. Although many residents are quick to point out that some of the media coverage of the Lower Ninth's social and physical isolation was deliberately misleading, most would agree that the neighbourhood suffered in a way that exemplified the shambles and scandals of post-Katrina reconstruction. Arnise Parker and Marie Hurt work for a local community campaign still fighting for the right of Lower Ninth residents to return to their homes. They confront a message from officialdom that says "Don't come back – there's nothing to come back to". Arnise is clear that what this really means is "Don't come back if you're poor or black". In the upheaval that followed the storm, while residents struggled with life and death, politicians and the development industry revealed a vision for the city's future with a cynicism that transcends conspiracy theories. Their plan excluded the people of the Lower Ninth and many others.

The exceptional nature of what happened in New Orleans in 2005 and its aftermath make direct comparisons difficult. But Arnise Parker's feeling is shared by people in other parts of the US, but also in the UK, where there's an increasing sense that urban regeneration projects are being used for social engineering. In the borough of Haringey in north London, the council is planning a 20-year programme to make Haringey "a place of great opportunity". To achieve this, publicly-owned housing, buildings and land are being packaged for transfer to a private joint venture company[123] which would have a turnover of at least £2 billion and increase land values by physically and socially transforming the area.[124] One of those fighting Haringey Council's plans, Paul Burnham, says:

> In the US, James Baldwin said 'urban renewal means negro removal' and we're seeing something similar here. We face social cleansing hiding in plain sight, and that has a racist impact. There are plenty of poor people of colour in Haringey: people the Council doesn't want around, at least not in such numbers. Driving up house prices means market forces push people out.

New Orwellian

Arnise and Marie realised the Lower Ninth faced a threat that was human not natural almost immediately after the storm passed. Even as the levees were breaking, there was talk of rebuilding the city with a "smaller footprint". Theories of urban planning based on compactness have abounded with growing awareness of the social and environmental damage of car-oriented suburban sprawl. Within a somewhat arcane debate about the "smart growth" of "walkable" and "liveable" cities, these concepts are often proxies for middle class aspirations. The extent to which superficial concern for the environment is used to justify profit-driven social engineering, was fully exposed in post-Katrina New Orleans. Wade Rathke, a community campaigner based in the area, argues that Lower Ninth residents knew for decades their neighbourhood was vulnerable to flooding. This was not because it's particularly low-lying (most of it isn't), but because commercial interests had exploited the Mississippi delta heedless of environmental damage, while

---

[123] The current "preferred bidder" is Lendlease, the same company that built the luxury *One57* block in New York City and is building private housing on formerly public land at the Heygate estate in south London.

[124] "Lives torn apart and assets lost: this is what a Labour privatisation would mean", Aditya Chakrabortty, *The Guardian*, 19th January 2017.

political interests had failed to adequately invest in flood defences since Hurricane Betsy in 1965.[125] Only after Katrina and the consequences of this neglect became apparent did the establishment begin to plan for a "sustainable" New Orleans. One way of achieving this was to abandon the Lower Ninth, or at least its pre-existing population. Questions about the extent to which the Lower Ninth was victim to wilful negligence persist. Marie Hurt has no doubt:

> Things were done deliberately. If you know you have a Category Five storm bearing down on you, you don't leave a big barge in the canal[126] because it will break the levy. They knew there wasn't enough protection.

The Lower Ninth was the last area to be drained of flood water and to which people were allowed to return. As soon as they did, they faced a new threat from city, Louisiana state and Federal authorities all working to demolish their homes. "No Bulldozing" signs appeared throughout the neighbourhood as wrecking crews, many of them out-of-town private contractors employing migrant labour, began trying to make it impossible for the Lower Ninth to be resettled. Access to and from the Lower Ninth was controlled by troops. The New Orleans director of Homeland Security, Terry Ebbert, surveying the area from a helicopter, said "nothing out there can be saved at all".[127] The city's mayor, Ray Nagin, with perhaps unintended candour, added "I don't think it can ever be what it was".[128] Marie thinks the Lower Ninth was partly being used as a "poster" to symbolise the extent of the disaster in the hope of attracting overdue government help. But she also thinks the ultimate intention was to use the hurricane to "wash away" the crime, poverty

---

[125] Rathke W (2011) *The Battle for the Ninth Ward: ACORN, rebuilding New Orleans, and the lesson of disaster*, New Orleans, Social Policy Press.

[126] This is a reference to an incident, recalled by many, in which a 200-foot barge left moored in the Industrial Canal during the storm crashed through the levee and into the Lower Ninth Ward.

[127] "Storm and Crisis: The overview; president visits as New Orleans sees some gains", *New York Times*, 12th September 2005.

[128] In 2014, Nagin was convicted of fraud and sentenced to ten years imprisonment.

and black people associated with the Lower Ninth, and create a blank slate for redevelopment.

Between 1852 and 1870, the city of Paris infamously combined wholesale urban redesign with mass clearance, demolition, displacement and coercion of working class neighbourhoods to create the quintessential bourgeois metropolis. As David Harvey[129] has described, the Parisian authorities bludgeoned into submission the communities in the path of redevelopment, as part of a fundamental social and economic reordering of the city that erased selected elements of its past. Something very similar was attempted by those who saw Katrina not as a human catastrophe, but a political and financial opportunity.

On the site of a slave market

The office of Southeast Louisiana Legal Services (SLLS) is on Common Street in New Orleans' central business district. For two centuries, the "central business" of New Orleans was buying and selling human beings and one of the main places for doing so was on Common Street. The slave trade literally and figuratively underlies the city's history and although it's trite to say this should never be forgotten, it often is. Establishing the causal link between slavery and enduring racism is difficult. Finding an organisation for social justice, SLLS, representing many people who are the descendants of slaves, on the site of a slave market is a salutary reminder of America's past and present.

Ten years on, SLLS is still dealing with the wreckage of Katrina, which its Executive Director Laura Tuggle describes, with measured under-statement, as "a game changer". While the legacy of the storm has been disproportionately felt by certain groups, its immediate impact was experienced by all in its path. The entire SLLS staff-team was temporarily displaced and over half lost their homes. The Common Street office was closed for ten weeks and

---

[129] Harvey D (2006) *Paris, Capital of Modernity*, London, Routledge.

several legal advisors left the organisation in the aftermath. Almost every advocate organisation in New Orleans and the surrounding area faced similar problems, and like others, SLLS was able to re-establish its operation relatively quickly. But disruption to the few agencies providing advice and support exacerbated the suffering for those most vulnerable to the unfolding crisis.

Arriving in the city on 11th June 2015 brought a noticeable contrast with other cities on my trip – an absence of people living and sleeping on the streets. SLLS confirmed this was a temporary phenomenon. There had recently been a "sweep". At regular intervals, the city authorities forcibly remove homeless people from their nooks under elevated freeways and in doorways. This happens whenever there's a high-profile "visitor attraction" happening, such as a New Orleans Saints football game or, on the weekend of 13/14 June, the Creole Tomato Festival! To make sure tourists aren't assailed by the poverty in their midst, according to SLLS, the police department gives homeless people a ten-minute warning to gather their belongings before using jet-washers to hose down the area where they'd been sleeping. The homeless are then herded towards a variety of hostels, some of which have a notorious reputation for Dickensian coercion and paternalism. Inevitably, with scant alternative permanent housing available, the homeless return. Sure enough, when the tomato festival was over, the spaces beneath Interstate 10, which slashes through the city, were festooned with cardboard shelters.

Just another homeless story

Tosheam Dudley told me his short story of homelessness when we met outside Tulane University Hospital, where he'd just had eight stitches in his head after being attacked by a fellow resident of his latest short-term hostel. Tosheam returned to New Orleans from New Jersey in 2009 to be reunited with his family. On the way he was arrested on charges of car theft. These were subsequently disproved, but Tosheam couldn't afford a lawyer at the time so was

Tosheam Dudley, with the papers for his next homeless shelter.

sentenced to one year, one month and one week in prison. (A feature of the punitive American penal system is its fondness for symbolic punishments.) After release, Tosheam entered the twilight existence of criminalised homelessness. At first he slept at Duncan Plaza, adjacent to City Hall, where he was later joined by the Occupy movement. Tosheam recalls being interviewed by a TV crew and saying "I ain't occupying nothing. I'm homeless!" Eventually, the encampment was "swept" and Tosheam moved to a series of New

Orleans shelters he described as rat-infested and "no place like home". When we met, Tosheam was on his way to see his public defence lawyer to discuss a variety of problems including the withdrawal of his food stamps. He was also trying to beg enough money for something to eat and the fare to his next homeless shelter in the Algiers district on the other side of the Mississippi. Tosheam had no idea if, or when, he would find permanent accommodation, but was full of hope for a time when he could get a job and be able to live with his partner and child in a home he would own. Tosheam's is just another homeless story from approximately 3.5 million in America each year. They're all different and all the same. This is a vast country with a very mobile population. The dynamics of displacement, dispersed kinship networks and economic necessity makes people accustomed to travelling long distances to find a better quality of life, a quest intrinsic to the American identity. This spirit of individual optimism and resourcefulness can be admirable, but also leaves a trail of victims, like Tosheam Dudley.

HANO

Before Katrina – and even more so after – alongside advocacy for the homeless a lot of SLLS' work was focused on tenants of the Housing Authority of New Orleans (HANO). Some mainstream political sympathy and support was eventually forthcoming for other constituencies of the flood-damaged city, but never reached public housing. The only high-profile exception was the UN Special Rapporteur on Housing, who called for an end to the demolition of little-damaged, but much-needed, public housing. Some of those who might have been expected to speak out on behalf of public housing, such as local African-American politicians, failed to do so and, indeed, became supporters of its privatisation. The course of public housing in New Orleans runs similar to other US cities, but as with everything post-Katrina, has attracted additional controversy. Since 2005, thousands of structurally-sound apartments, the homes of some of the city's poorest people, most of them African-

American, have been demolished to make way for income-specific, privatised "mixed" communities. In a simple but profound message, in the aftermath of Katrina, some public housing tenants visited a wealthy area of New Orleans with a banner reading "MAKE THIS NEIGHBOURHOOD MIXED INCOME".[130]

The view of many housing campaigners in the city is that Katrina both accelerated demolition and divestment and provided a smoke-screen of justification for them. In most other places, such decisions were taken by locally appointed Public Housing Authorities (PHAs) with at least a modicum of municipal accountability, although there was a clear intention to follow national HUD policy. In New Orleans, the federal government cut out the middle-man. Ostensibly because of mismanagement, HANO had been under direct HUD control since the early 2000s. There are numerous examples of local PHAs being taken over by HUD in the wake of incompetence or corruption, but in New Orleans it became unambiguous that the remodelling of the city without public housing was a direct order from Washington DC.

Remote control

The imposition of central government control over local public housing highlights another important aspect of US-UK convergence. Allowing for their administrative differences, both US public housing and UK council housing were established with a degree of local accountability and democratic legitimacy. The link between elected politicians and municipal housing is more direct in Britain and has motivated many of the ideological attacks upon it. The post-1979 Tory government was quite explicit that it saw breaking up council housing as a way of undermining the Labour Party.[131] Strangely, subsequent Labour governments continued the assault!

---

[130] "Survivor's Village Marches on Garden District', *neworleans.indymedia.org*, 17th June 2006.

[131] Stoker G (1988) *The Politics of Local Government*, (pp 177 – 182), London, Macmillan Education.

Academic and policy critics argued that making access to housing a "political issue" led to abuse of power, and advocated the replacement of directly elected landlords with the appointed boards of housing associations, a model that resembles the governance structure of US public housing although both still tend to have politically connected representatives.[132]

Weakening the link between local housing and the local ballot box and a shift towards remote control by central government as in the US has been a feature of UK policy since 1979. There was some superficial wavering of this line under the post-2010 Coalition government which introduced "self-financing" as a way of allowing local Councils more autonomy. But the underlying trajectory of increasing central government control is confirmed by the post-2015 Conservative government imposing compulsory rent cuts on local authorities and seeking to compel them to sell off the most valuable council homes. Imposing government policy by diktat has been crucial in achieving the slow-motion erosion of decent, secure, affordable housing, experienced in fast-forward in New Orleans.

Net losses

In 1996, HANO owned and managed 13,000 homes, housing 20 per cent of the city's African-American community. By August 2005 the ravages of HOPE VI had reduced this to 7,200, of which 2,000 stood empty pending redevelopment. Since Katrina, another 3,000 have been demolished at the city's four biggest public housing sites. They were eventually replaced with 1,829 new, privately-owned homes, of which less than half were at public housing rent levels. Despite a promised "right to return", very few tenants did so. For example, at the St Bernard project (later renamed Columbia Parc), in 2005 there were 963 homes, in 2015 there were 229, of which only 107 were occupied by former tenants. Similar losses – and rebranding – took place at the other big HANO sites C J Peete (now

---

[132] Although it should be noted that the 2016 Housing and Planning Act frees housing associations from having locally elected politicians sit on their Boards.

Harmony Oaks), Lafitte (Faubourg Lafitte) and B W Cooper (Marrero Commons). The remaining HANO stock is currently undergoing "comprehensive regeneration" and privatisation under the familiar guise of the Choice Neighbourhoods Initiative (CNI) programme. However, in another recurring pattern, while the number of permanent homes has reduced by almost two-thirds, the number of housing vouchers distributed by HANO has doubled to 18,000. During the post-Katrina period, the waiting list for public housing rose from 22,000 to 33,000. Although this was substantially reduced by the number of people leaving the city and not returning, the list still stood at 18,000 in 2015 and was closed for new applicants so is certainly an underestimate of need.

Destruction by design

The wholesale destruction of New Orleans' public housing once again exposes the lie that such decisions are based on design or technical considerations.[133] HANO's low-rise, modestly-scaled, pitched roofed public housing had been described by architectural critic Nicolai Ouroussoff as some of the best in the United States:

> Solidly built, the buildings' detailed brickwork, tile roofs and wrought-iron balustrades represent a level of craft more likely found on an Ivy League campus than in a contemporary public housing complex.[134]

150,000 New Orleans homes were destroyed or seriously damaged by the storm and the flooding that followed, of which 80 per cent were lived in by low-income renters. But damage to the city's public housing was minimal. In evidence to a legal challenge against the demolition of the Big Four HANO developments, John Fernandez, a professor of architecture at Massachusetts Institute of Technology, testified that having inspected a sample of homes there was,

---

[133] For a meticulous account of New Orleans public housing pre- and post- Katrina, the work of Bill Quigley (https://billquigley.wordpress.com/) is recommended.

[134] "All Fall Down", *New York Times*, 19th November 2006.

...no structural or non-structural damage...that would reasonably warrant any cost-effective building demolition....justifications for demolition on the grounds that these buildings can no longer function as safe and humane housing for the people of New Orleans are not credible.

Such independent evidence is rarely, if ever, admitted to the process of deciding the future of public or council housing. Instead, tenants facing the loss of their homes are presented with reports suggesting only one option is really under consideration. The dissemination of unbalanced information leads to false economies. HANO's internal documents show that it would have been far cheaper to repair and improve its housing than knock it down. For example, the 900 homes at the Lafitte development could have been repaired for $20 million and fully refurbished for $85 million, while the cost of demolition and rebuilding significantly fewer homes was over $100 million. Similar questions about decisions to demolish, instead of refurbish council housing have been raised in the UK.[135]

One of the real reasons why New Orleans' vital supply of permanent public housing was a target, both before and after Katrina, is that most of its tenants were black and poor. Moreover, New Orleans public housing – perhaps to an even greater degree than in other US cities – had been closely identified with African-American political activism. In the late 1960s and early 1970s, the Desire housing development was the focal point of a campaign, led by the Black Panthers, for social justice and against police brutality. In the early 1980s, tenants at the St Thomas site organised a prolonged and successful rent strike, demanding better conditions and opposing cuts in benefit payments. HANO tenants fiercely and successfully opposed attempts to demolish public housing in the late 80s. Such examples illustrate a recurring role of public housing as a seat of political and cultural resistance to prevailing capitalist norms. This truth was chillingly exposed by Louisiana Congressman

---

[135] "Demolition or Refurbishment of Social Housing: A review of the evidence", University College London, October 2014.

Richard Baker in the days after Katrina when he said "We finally cleaned up public housing in New Orleans. We couldn't do it, but God did."[136]

For Baker and his class, Katrina was a perfect storm for advancing neoliberal housing and urban policy. Tenants in other parts of the US and UK fear that if a similar catastrophe befell their area, the vultures of privatisation would respond in the same way.

Iberville-Treme

The inflated cost of demolition and redevelopment may be one reason why many of the lost HANO homes have not been replaced, as promised. This relates to the wider scandal of the authorities' selective failure to rebuild New Orleans. One of the places awaiting "cleaning up" is the Iberville public housing development in the Treme district, just north-west of the famed French Quarter. It is, therefore, one of the most potentially lucrative property development sites in the city. Following the razing of 821 homes (some of the original 1940s blocks have been preserved and are on the National Register of Historic Places) HANO pledged a vaguely defined "one for one" replacement on the site and an additional 1,500 new homes on "scattered sites" within the neighbourhood as part of another Choice Neighbourhood Initiative (CNI) project. The projected budget was $662 million, with HUD funding of $30.5 million intended to attract the remaining money from the private sector to build the new homes and "revitalise" the entire area.

With typical flights of rhetoric, HUD announced that Choice Neighbourhoods would promote a "safer, better-educated community with the tools its residents need to achieve self-sufficiency". Congressman Cedric Richmond invoked the US Constitution saying the CNI project would "help folks fully access their rights to life, liberty, and the pursuit of happiness" and President Obama added "we'll win the future only if we can ensure that people in every

---

[136] "Clamouring to come home to New Orleans projects", *New York Times*, 6th June 2006.

community – even those living in our most troubled neighbourhoods – have access to the American Dream."[137] So far, the dream
has failed.

As of mid-2015, 228 homes had been completed at Iberville-
Treme, rebranded as Bienville Basin. With typical salami-slicing of
public housing, 43 per cent were for market rent, 21 per cent were
"affordable workforce housing" and only 36 per cent were nomi-
nally "public". Monthly market rents were advertised at $1,250 for
one bedroom and $1,500 for two, significantly above the New
Orleans average. A further 269 homes are due to be completed at
Iberville-Treme by 2017, still substantially less than the target and
with the promised replacement public housing only making up 30
per cent of each phase of the scheme. A local journalist, Katy Reckdahl, has calculated that at the current rate of progress the project
won't be completed until 2026! There is additional local controversy about the off-site homes, very few of which have been built.
Confirming that all is not well with the Iberville-Treme CNI project,
the Executive Director of HANO, Gregg Fortner, has been quoted
as saying of the original plan "you can throw it out of the window".
Being exact about numbers of new homes, tenure-splits and ownership is difficult because HANO and their private sector development partners are reluctant to provide full details.[138]

Destructive accounting

The obfuscation and manipulation of figures, particularly relating
to non-market homes, has become standard procedure within the
property industry. Public authorities are complicit in restricting
access to information. A variety of barriers, including ambiguous
definitions of "affordable", contrived claims of "commercial confi-
dentiality", labyrinthine procedures, spinning PR operations and
failure to monitor exactly what gets built, all conspire to obscure

---

[137] HUD press release, 1st September 2011.
[138] Katy Reckdahl "10 Years After Katrina, New Orleans Public Housing Still in Limbo",
Next City, 15th June 2015.

the true nature of profit-driven developments. Often hard-pressed municipal planning departments struggle with the pace of new development and their ability to scrutinise adequately is compromised by pressure to attract and facilitate investment and growth. In addition, there is the bureaucratic instinct to close ranks when projects are struggling to deliver on commitments, particularly in an intense political climate such as post-2005 New Orleans.

Even in less dramatic circumstances, an unholy alliance of developers, policy-makers and politicians often frustrate the legitimate demands of tenants and campaigners wanting transparency and accountability about the use of public land and money. The UK's high-profile Greenwich Millennium Village (GMV) project in south-east London, for example, has been subject to numerous delays and controversies. In an area with an acute shortage of genuinely affordable housing, the local authority failed to keep accurate data about how many non-market homes were being built by private developers, on formerly publicly-owned land acquired with £180 million of government funding. This is typical where a coalition of vested interests operates to hide the truth of what is getting built – and who for.

Supping with the PPP

The Iberville-Treme and GMV experiences further illustrate concerns about the role of "public–private partnerships" which, though intensified in New Orleans, are by no means unique to it. At one level, there is nothing new about private business involvement in urban redevelopments. This has been a feature of housing policy on both sides of the Atlantic since governments first got involved in building homes. What has changed over the last generation is a new consensus among the political and policy establishment that improving the conditions of urban working class neighbourhoods is impossible without "partnership".

There is a strong ideological momentum for this orthodoxy based on the unproved assumption that the private sector is "better" than the public. But the true motivation is financial. Large-scale regeneration projects bring access to government money, political patronage and above all, public land. Since the public private partnership shift in the early 1980s, countless (because nobody is counting!) acres of land and other valuable assets have been transferred from public ownership to the private sector. Examples are too numerous to list, but the wholesale disposal of 6,000 acres of London's disused docks in 1981 established a template and an accompanying language replicated ad nauseam since. Based on a contrived narrative that the area had become a "forgotten wasteland", Margaret Thatcher's Conservative government imposed a redevelopment agency, the London Docklands Development Corporation (LDDC), which effectively annexed an area of 8.5 square miles previously administered by three democratically mandated municipal authorities. The LDDC assumed direct planning and decision-making powers, including the disposal of publically-owned land and use of £1.86 billion of government funding. Hundreds of council homes were bulldozed to make way for a new road, but local "communities" (a relatively novel policy term at the time) were minimally compensated with a time-limited budget for local facilities and projects. Very few of the 24,000 new homes built under the LDDC were affordable to people originally living in the area. This use of public private partnership to achieve total physical, economic and social domination in the image of global capitalism has spawned numerous imitations.

Sister Christine Frost has been at the heart of struggles for social justice and secure housing in the Docklands area since the LDDC arrived. She reflects:

> Typical of Margaret Thatcher's era was a promise of "trickle down", which would supposedly allow local communities to share the wealth from Docklands. We're still waiting! The community isn't against change, but we want to share the benefits. Instead we're being squeezed out of the area.

Fit and proper people?

One of the private sector partners at Iberville-Treme is HRI Properties,[139] whose mission statement is "revitalising cities by creating diverse, vibrant and sustainable communities". HRI's portfolio is valued at $1.5 billion and includes hotels, luxury apartments and offices. A former New Orleans mayor, Sidney Barthelemy, is a company senior executive and a former employee was Vince Lane, agent of public housing privatisation in Chicago (until his imprisonment for fraud). Before Katrina, the company was involved in the redevelopment of the 1,500-home St Thomas HANO site, demolished in 2000. As at Iberville-Treme, displaced public housing tenants were promised a "right to return" to the rebranded River Garden, but only 100 did so, some of them only after taking legal action against HANO. Alongside 600 ubiquitous HOPE VI "mixed income" homes, among the new occupants of the neighbourhood is a Walmart. Council tenants in the UK will be very familiar with the use of a chain-supermarket store to "anchor" the reshaping of their community, often at the expense of long-established local, family-run shops.

Another of the private companies involved in Iberville-Treme is McCormack Baron Salazar (MBS), a St Louis-based firm of self-styled "ethical" property developers of the kind that has gained increasing prominence – and profits – since public-private partnerships became the norm of urban regeneration. MBS describes itself as "the nation's leading for-profit developer of economically integrated urban neighbourhoods" and has been involved in several HOPE VI and Choice Neighbourhood projects around the US. It has a housing portfolio worth $3 billion spread across 38 US cities. An indication of MBS's growing wealth is that in May 2010, global finance company Goldman Sachs acquired a one-third stake in the company. MBS is also part of an institutional network of academics, policy-makers and private businesses – some with direct UK links

---

[139] Abbreviated from "Historic Restoration Incorporated".

– that collaborates around a shared cause of "improving" urban neighbourhoods by destroying public housing. Two of MBS's founding members, Terry McCormack and Richard Baron, were involved in the process – which began as advocacy on behalf of tenants – that eventually led to the demolition of Pruitt-Igoe in St Louis, the catalyst for US public housing's denigration and decline.

The third sector

The Iberville-Treme partnership also highlights the insidious role of the "third sector" and "non-profits" in advancing the cause of privatisation. A spider's web of agencies and professionals accompanies the awarding of large amounts of public money to deprived areas. At least 15 different organisations are involved in the Iberville-Treme CNI, pledging $24.5 million in funding, although this is mostly "in kind".[140] These intermediaries stand between local residents and direct access to the funding allocated to their areas, with spending decisions taken by incorporated and often unelected bodies. Local residents are represented in some form, but never have a controlling majority. This model of superimposed community development and leadership has become routine within contemporary US and UK urban policy. The UK equivalent of Choice Neighbourhoods, New Deal for Communities (NDC), was re-named by residents from one NDC area "new deal for consultants" because of the proliferation of third sector agencies who siphon-off money intended for housing and social facilities.[141] Working alongside McCormack Baron Salazar at Iberville-Treme is Urban Strategies Inc, a national "non-profit" organisation, also based in St Louis, founded in 1978 and dedicated to working specifically with public housing communities. Richard Baron and another representative of MBS are on the Urban Strategies board of directors, as is a vice-

---

[140] "In kind" funding represents the projected costs of an organisation for being involved in a project.

[141] Robbins G (2002) *Taking Stock – Regeneration Programme and Social Housing* in Local Economy Vol. 17, no. 4, pp266-272.

president of Goldman Sachs. Urban Strategies helped pioneer the "holistic" approach to urban regeneration that has become another unquestioned tenet in the urban regeneration canon, with dubious motives and results, however laudable the original intentions. In New Orleans, Urban Strategies secured lucrative contracts to advance the wider social aims of Choice Neighbourhoods. The focus was through "capacity building" in the form of training and awarding small grants to local community groups through a competitive – and inherently divisive – bidding process.

The "third sector" is a blanket term for a broad range of entities, from genuinely voluntary, locally-based community groups with few resources, to what are effectively private businesses with big budgets, highly paid executives with little or no connection with the neighbourhood they're seeking to work in. The web of relationships and motivations in State-led, bureaucratised urban regeneration is made more complex by the existence, particularly in the US but increasingly in the UK, of professionalised activism. Originating from the distinctive American political culture, in which challenges to the establishment have struggled for mainstream representation, opposition movements have developed in a particular form in which autonomous groups play a significant role. This model contrasts with the more staid UK tradition usually mediated and articulated (at least for most of the 20th century) through the labour and trade union movement. The work of Saul Alinsky[142] and his philosophy of pragmatic, tactical and conditional engagement with State funding agencies, has been influential in developing a model of activism based on the maxim "if you're not round the table, you're on the menu". A myriad of US organisations, some with national reach, has emerged from this allegedly anti-ideological pool to become significant players in urban improvement projects. They act as advocates, sometimes successfully, for the demands of local

---

[142] Alinsky S D (1971) *Rules for Radicals: A pragmatic primer for realistic radicals*, New York, Vintage Books.

people. But they can also end up conforming to the language and agenda of those controlling the purse-strings.

Activist and academic John Arena[143] spent many years campaigning alongside tenants and other social justice groups in New Orleans and has chronicled how the "non-profit industrial complex" played an active role in the "betrayal" and privatisation of public housing, both before and after Katrina. He records how some of the people most incorporated by the partnership model had previously been among the most active defenders of public housing and independent tenant-led organisations. A similar pattern has been a feature of regeneration projects leading to the privatisation of council housing in the UK. Arena argues that involvement in third sector organisations serves the dual purpose of promoting alignment and conformity with the dominant policy structure, while sapping and canalising political energy that might otherwise challenge it.

It's easy to condemn individuals who "sell out" by identifying themselves with officialdom and policies that undermine the long-term interests of working class communities. Whatever the personal motivations, it's important to balance these alongside the cumulative pressures imposed on poor neighbourhoods starved of investment for years. As in the case of stock transfer in the UK, it is difficult to criticise tenants who've been told they will be consigned to sub-standard living conditions unless they accept the strings of privatisation attached to the promise of funding and improvements. Condemnation belongs to the bribery, not the bribed. Account must also be taken of the relentless nature of privatisation forces. New Orleans public housing had been under constant attack for decades before an alliance converged that instigated its destruction, a process that Katrina completed. Self-organised working class campaigns of resistance often struggle to sustain involvement across the prolonged time-scales that governmental and corporate inter-

---

[143] Arena J (2012)*Driven from New Orleans: How non-profits betray public housing and promote privatisation*, Minneapolis, University of Minnesota Press.

ests are able to maintain. This can lead to the search for short-cuts and an instinct to accept the "bird in the hand".

Resident management

Another element of the apparently disparate, ultimately coalescing forces enabling the privatisation of public housing is resident management.[144] The complex and often contradictory issues involved were again amplified in New Orleans. Like other non-profits, Resident Management Organisations (RMOs)[145] are often presented in uncritical terms. This is justified by the fact that they are, by definition, led by residents themselves, albeit that their creation may be significantly influenced by external forces. The origins of resident management lie in attempts, in both the US and UK, to find local solutions to the allegedly institutional and intractable problems of managing public/council housing. On both sides of the Atlantic – and with a significant degree of policy cross-pollination – from the 1970s in the US (somewhat later in the UK) an almost evangelical movement developed around the proposition that the best people to take responsibility for the upkeep of their homes and communities were the people who lived in them. Beguiling stories of bootstrap self-help and sleeves-rolled up practicality elevate the status of certain individuals, while concealing the practical difficulties of resident management, its political function, divisiveness and the fact that it is always a defensive manoeuvre. It is invariably the result of resignation on the part of tenants at the failures of statutory authorities to provide the level of service to which they're entitled. One RMO was established in New Orleans in 1988 at the Guste public housing development. In a familiar story, its leader became a high-profile figure courted by establishment politi-

---

[144] In the interests of disclosure, at the time of writing the author works for a resident management organisation in the UK and has worked for several others in the past.

[145] Resident management has various guises. In the US, it commonly takes the form of Resident Management Corporations (RMCs); in the UK, Tenant Management Organisations or Cooperatives (TMO/Cs).

cians, failed to align herself with campaigns to oppose the privatisation of other HANO homes, and has subsequently been criticised
in the local media for the scale of her salary and the fact that other
members of her family are also employed by the RMO. Similar
issues have been associated with resident management in the UK,
where Tenant Management Organisations have often been muted
in their opposition to council house privatisation and sometimes
complicit in it.

The expectation, often fostered by well-paid external consultants,
that public/council housing tenants should "participate" in the
management of their homes is another form of discriminatory
paternalism imposed on working class communities and is also a
direct route to incorporation. Resident management does have the
potential to be a positive and effective adjunct to housing services,
but like other features of the "non-profit industrial complex" has
often become a tool in the hands of those fundamentally hostile to
public or municipal housing.

From housing and beyond

Critics of top-down regeneration programmes administered via
public private partnerships and the third sector have warned they
can become an engine for a wider privatisation agenda, beyond
housing. This tendency has been particularly pronounced in the
US, but is also creeping into the UK. Some UK housing associations, for example, are involved in the setting up of
Academy/Charter Schools and are also bidding for public sector
contracts in other fields.

The perfect neoliberal storm of Katrina once again revealed the
extent of the privatisation offensive and the opportunist ruthless-
ness with which its advocates are prepared to pursue it. Charity
Hospital, a short walk from Iberville-Treme, was, until three weeks
after Katrina, one of the longest-functioning and largest public
hospitals in the US, dating back to the 1730s. The latest building
was completed in 1939 as part of the New Deal Public Works

Administration: in addition to its social role, it is a magnificent example of art-deco architecture. But the opportunity to close Charity Hospital using the excuse of storm damage was too good to miss for politicians and developers. By doing so they gained control of another valuable city-centre site and removed another symbol of social welfare.[146]

Another partner in the Iberville-Treme CNI was Lagniappe Academies, a private Charter school company which committed $3.4 million to the programme in 2011. US Charter schools, broadly similar to UK Academies, are quasi-public (they may receive some public funding), but often owned by private, profit-making businesses, some with numerous institutions under their control. US public schools (not to be confused with the elitist British institutions of the same name) have transcended some of the American prejudice against State services and are a corner-stone of many communities. But public schools are under threat in many cities, where they are associated with a broader, covertly racialised, image of urban decay. Campaigners in Chicago's South Side tell how the closure of public schools compounded the disruption of community infrastructure caused by the destruction of public housing. A similar pattern emerged in New Orleans. The city's education system was particularly hard-hit by Katrina. As with housing, some identified an opportunity in adversity. Before the storm there were 124 schools in the city, most of them administered by the local municipality. Only eight were Charter schools. After Katrina, there were 83 schools, of which 76 were Charters.[147] The city's 7,000 teachers were all dismissed after Katrina and compelled to reapply for jobs, often with new employers and under new, non-union negotiated terms and conditions. As in housing, an ethnic restructuring also took place, with many black teachers from the city replaced with white

---

[146] "Why was New Orleans's Charity Hospital Allowed to Die?", *The Nation*, 27th April 2011.

[147] "Hope, resentment in New Orleans' charter school landscape", *The Times-Picayune*, 20th August 2014.

teachers from somewhere else.[148] However, Lagniappe Academies will not be part of New Orleans' new education world, or of the putative Iberville-Treme transformation. They closed down in May 2015, creating more uncertainty about the public private partnership model in general and the future of the Iberville-Treme CNI in particular.

Unions

Sadly, trade unions were another ingredient in the toxic brew infecting post-Katrina New Orleans. The role of organised labour marks another important contrast between housing struggles in the US and UK. Although unions have historically held a more prominent position in British politics and society, they have been less involved in non-workplace and community-based mobilisations than their US counterparts. This is reflected, for example, in the direct provision of co-operative housing in New York and on-going engagement with a broad range of civic organisations and campaigns, sometimes with ulterior financial motives.

Unions played a contradictory role in opposing privatisation of New Orleans public housing, combining opposition with accommodation, particularly when lucrative construction contracts were in the offing. Similar tensions are latent elsewhere, such as the Bronx, where rank and file union members have been involved in opposition to the re-zoning of the Cromwell-Jerome corridor while union leaders are anxious to ensure that any rebuilding work employs union labour with union rates of pay. While this may be a legitimate position for unions seeking to represent their members, it undermines trusting alliances with wider forces, including tenants who are likely to have incomes significantly below union rates and be more directly affected by the results of redevelopment. Such conflicts of interest become entrenched by the increasing bureau-

---

[148] As of February 2017, a process to return New Orleans' charter schools to public control was underway. "Final votes begin to return New Orleans schools to local control", *The Times-Picayune*, 14th February 2017.

cratisation and detachment of trade union leadership, a process in which the UK is rapidly catching up with the US. Dr Ian MacDonald, a researcher in industrial relations at the University of Montreal, has suggested that American trade unions have themselves been incorporated into the neoliberal project.[149] Although some unions have played an important role in resisting housing privatisation, there was a similar shift towards "new realism" in the UK labour movement since the late 1980s, a period coinciding with the intensifying assault on council housing.

However, alongside the questionable role of union bosses in perpetuating crony relationships with employers and politicians, must be set the naked attack on unions that was another feature of post-Katrina New Orleans. At a time of turmoil and with huge salvage and rebuilding contracts to be won, employers, with government support, used every mechanism to undercut pay and conditions. Appalling stories of hyper-exploitation, particularly of migrant labour, emerged during the clear-up operation, reinforcing the prevailing racism and profiteering that characterised what happened after the storm.

Culture clash

Some aspects of post-Katrina attacks on public housing and other mainstays of working class New Orleans community life raise deeper issues than rents, jobs and wages. The HBO TV series Treme attempts to capture, albeit in a somewhat romanticised fashion, the unique character of the area currently facing a corporate-led makeover to become an "urban village". The Treme is one of the oldest communities of free African-Americans in the US, where a fusion of ethnicities has produced an urban culture and landscape with few parallels. Jazz and Cajun food are internationally known, but here they connect with a local history and identity now threatened

---

[149] MacDonald I T (2014) *Towards Neoliberal Trade Unionism: Decline, renewal and transformation in north American labour movements,* British Journal of Industrial Relations, Vol. 52, issue 4, December 2014.

by redevelopment. One life-long New Orleanian recalled to me the sad incongruity of seeing a Mardi Gras Indian parade taking place where a HANO site had been replaced with the fake urbanity of mixed income housing and a Big Box retail park. The elaborate feathered costumes of the Indians commemorate the folk traditions of one people already obliterated by imperialism. The continuing assault on New Orleans' working class neighbourhoods threatens those of another.

A political and business elite wanted to repackage the culture of New Orleans by fundamentally restructuring its economy and demographic, but it didn't work. Resistance took many forms and as in the case of public housing, was not always successful. But the determination of people to return to their homes has been typified by the Lower Ninth and is summed up by local resident Arnise Parker:

> The anger stays within. Katrina and what happened after it are always on your mind. We've never had a real account of the people who died – and are still dying. My pastor was burying two or three people a week. Being black has always been a struggle, but especially in New Orleans. But people love the city and that's why they came back.

Politically and commercially-motivated rumours of the city's death proved exaggerated. Despite the many obstacles, from delayed insurance payments and dramatic rent rises to the closure of local schools and hospitals, New Orleans has recovered most of its pre-Katrina population, albeit that some of the new inhabitants weren't living in the city a decade ago. Arnise and many other campaigners are involved in projects to help the repopulation of the Lower Ninth by the people who left it. The corner-stone is re-establishing the area's tradition of working class home-ownership. While many US and UK housing campaigns rightly focus their attention on improving conditions in the rental sector, experience in the Lower Ninth is an important reminder that we are not only fighting for tenants' rights. Home owners too can be part of the struggle to assert the right for working class people to live in the cities they built.

Conclusions

Almost any comment about the impact of Hurricane Katrina on New Orleans, especially from an outsider, is destined for understatement. In Spike Lee's epic 2006 documentary *When the Levees Broke*, one resident, of many who experienced forced displacement, privation, discrimination, violence and the separation of their families, compared the storm's aftermath to some of the conditions of slavery. While thousands of people faced the loss of their lives, livelihoods and homes, a few others saw a commercial opportunity.

Some of the pronouncements from politicians and big business in the days after 29th August 2005 beggar belief. President George W Bush was widely criticised for his slow and inept response to the disaste. His mother, Barbara Bush, in a 21st century imitation of Marie Antoinette, said on a visit to an evacuee shelter in Texas, "so many of the people in the arena here, you know, were underprivileged anyway so this is working very well for them."[150]

The extent of the American establishment's involvement in the attempt to re-build New Orleans to a corporate design is confirmed by Barbara Bush's ex-President husband sitting alongside private property developers on the board of one of the non-profit companies "revitalising" the St Bernard's public housing development. Katrina unleashed political and policy cynicism on a grotesque scale, to create what is almost a biblical parable exposing the truth of neoliberalism and its determination to control, consume and commodify everything in its path. A particular facet of this operation was the removal of public housing which, as John Arena says, represented "an obstacle to the full spatial, cultural, political and economic emergence and maintenance of the neoliberal city, which could only be achieved by clearing the ground of poor people".

---

[150] "Barbara Bush Calls Evacuees Better Off", *New York Times*, 7th September 2005.

While people of all ethnicities suffered, Katrina exposed, once again, the enduring racism at the heart of American housing and urban policy. The "deconcentration" of poor African-Americans from their inner-city homes to make way for a more affluent and white population is evident throughout the nation. It assumed additional velocity in post-Katrina New Orleans, as recounted by local resident and musician Davis Rogan:[151] "The city since Katrina has been substantially blanched. The poor and the black didn't get to come back. Thirty years of gentrification has happened in ten".

---

[151] A character based on Davis Rogan features in the HBO *Treme* series.

7

The Atlanta way

Introduction

The US housing crisis is national in scale, but local in character. The situation in different cities reflects their particular history, culture and social dynamics. Atlanta is a city whose destruction in 1864 – immortalised in *Gone with Wind* – symbolised the end of the Old South and its "peculiar institution" of slavery. Atlanta is also sometimes known as "the capital of the civil rights movement". These polarising but related historic images find physical and political expression in contemporary Atlanta, and appear to distance the city from its past. Like its 19th century predecessor, central Atlanta has been gutted, this time by an army of property developers using an arsenal of weapons aimed at the usual targets: working class, predominantly African-American communities and public housing. An aggressive encircling of downtown Atlanta has been prosecuted using mega-events, sports-stadiums, university campus expansions and mixed use commercial developments, to create a corporate enclave at the heart of the city. This alienating urban landscape literally covers up some of Atlanta's old streets, which are preserved in a bizarre subterranean parody.[152]

In his 1998 novel *A Man in Full*,[153] Tom Wolfe captures the transformation of Atlanta through the eyes of a speculative property developer against the background of high-rise office blocks, exclusive private clubs and obsession with sport. In one passage Wolfe's main protagonist, Charlie Croker, looks down on the city from his private jet and expresses the messianic, ego-mania of his type:

> Many was the time that the view from up here looking down upon the towers and the trees, had filled him with an inexpressible joy. "I did that! That's my handiwork! I'm one of the giants who built this city!"

The towers Wolfe describes exemplify the growing gap between America's rich and poor. This is at its widest in Atlanta where, in

---

[152] At "Atlanta Underground" in the city centre, authentic post-Civil War/Reconstruction-era buildings that were built under viaducts supporting first railways and then roads, have been incorporated into a shopping mall.

[153] Wolfe T (1998) *A Man in Full*, New York, Bantam Books.

2015, the richest five per cent had an average income of $288,159, the poorest 20 per cent only $14,988. While Atlanta may not have the same influx of extreme wealth as Seattle or San Francisco, the city's political economy is dominated by a mega-rich establishment, some of which trace its origins to the pre-Civil War South. It includes one of the great symbols of American capitalism, Coca-Cola, which was first sold in Atlanta in 1886. A regime of business-political leadership is characterised by what Professor Larry Keating from Georgia Tech University describes as "the ability of a corporate elite to mobilise political and fiscal resources behind specific projects."[154]

Adventures of a slum fighter

An Atlanta plutocrat was responsible for one of America's first public housing schemes,[155] directly inspired by UK practice. Charles Palmer was a property developer whose daily drives from the Atlanta suburbs to his office took him through the city's Tech Flats slum, an experience which inspired him to seek solutions to urban poverty.[156] This quest took Palmer to London in the mid-1930s, where he witnessed the squalor of the East End and its anticipated antidote. He visited the Becontree council estate which enabled 25,000 families (including mine) to exchange the sub-standard conditions and insecurity of unregulated private renting for the inter-generational benefits of a decent, secure, affordable home. Becontree's cottage-style, brick-built housing with front and back gardens and generous open space was the inspiration Palmer brought back to Atlanta for Techwood Homes.

His motivation probably included a degree of enlightened self-interest. Tech Flats was very close to some of Palmer's valuable land-

---

[154] Keating L (2001) *Atlanta: Race, Class and Urban Expansion*, Philadelphia, Temple University Press.

[155] New York claims the First Houses development, which was first occupied on 3rd December 1935, as the original US public housing, but Techwood Homes in Atlanta can also claim the title based on it having a greater degree of direct central, rather than local, government investment.

[156] Palmer C F (1955) *Adventures of a Slum Fighter*, Atlanta, Tupper and Love.

holdings. He concluded "it costs more to keep slums than to clear them" and began a crusade to convince US politicians of the need for public housing. He met a receptive audience in President Roosevelt's Public Works Administration. The government agreed to provide funding to replace Tech Flats with new model homes, for which the President himself switched on the electricity on 29th November 1935. The policy met fierce resistance from private property developers and landlords, worried about the threat to their profits. Atlanta Real Estate Board president G M "Tommy" Stout raised objections couched in disingenuous, racialised and ideological terms that ring down the years and across oceans:

> The working class will rue the day when they are housed in government owned, government built and government regulated houses. Masters house their slaves, but free men house themselves. Those who are descendants of pioneer American stock will not regard as "home" a unit in a fine building built at tax-payers' expense... There are very powerful motives that stir people to action. One is self-interest. In ordinary times this is the motive which dominates.

Despite the hostile real estate lobby, Techwood Homes created 2,000 jobs and decent housing for 604 families. As ever, this did not include many of the 1,611 families displaced by the clearance of Tech Flats, of which 28 per cent were African-American. Ignoring a 1917 Supreme Court judgment, Atlanta had introduced segregationist residential zoning rules in the early 1920s, and the new Techwood Homes were exclusively for whites. Nonetheless, Techwood Homes once more confounded popular myths around public housing (at least until falling victim to HOPE VI and the Olympics in the early 1990s). Reflecting the expansive vision of Palmer and other 1930s housing reformers, the development comprised low-rise brick-built buildings set among landscaped gardens and playgrounds with local shops, a communal laundrette, health clinic, library and on-site housing management office. Techwood Homes set the standard for the first phase of US public housing, enshrined in the 1937 Housing Act, but remained "whites only" until the late 1960s, mounting pressure from the civil rights movement for desegregation. Then a growing population of African-Americans living in the city centre caused alarm to corporate Atlanta, including Coca-Cola whose chief executive started lobbying for demolition in the early 1970s. This initial threat was seen off by a new generation of elected black politicians. But the relentless privatisation machine continued to roll and prevailed 25 years later when Atlanta was awarded the 1996 Olympics.

Centennial Place

The Olympic assault successfully fended-off by the people of Boston in 2015 was felt with full force by Atlanta. When the Games were awarded to the city in 1990, redevelopment plans that had simmered for decades came to the boil. Global big business has established a formula for reshaping cities, fuelled by the hyperbolic feel-good rhetoric of mega-sports events. The 1996 Olympics presented a golden opportunity for property developers, civic boosters and politicians to realise their "vision" for central Atlanta to become the financial centre of the South. Techwood Homes and the adjoining Clark Howell Homes – 1,195 affordable homes in total – did not fit with this glittering image. These homes were explicitly referred to by supporters of the Games as a potential embarrassment to international visitors and investors. An executive of Georgia Tech University, one of the key privateers, described Techwood Homes as a "cesspool". Atlanta public housing tenants had successfully defended their homes in the past, but were now confronted by a co-ordinated attack, pioneering tactics now commonplace in the US and UK.

The condition of Techwood and Clark Howell Homes had been allowed to deteriorate for a decade (since most of their residents became African-American). Literally thousands of repairs were outstanding. Wilful mismanagement and neglect is a recurring and deliberate strategy of housing privatisation. The cumulative failure to carry out repairs, maintenance and caretaking has physical, political and psychological effects, creating a climate of despair and frustration and making it easier to present privatisation as the only solution. Alongside the allure of the Olympics, the newly-introduced HOPE VI initiative beguiled public housing tenants with a message that this was a "once in a lifetime" opportunity. The executive director of the Atlanta Housing Authority (AHA), Renee Lewis Glover – annual salary in 2010 $644,000, even described HOPE VI as "God given". This form of arm-twisting by over-paid public employees was routinely used in the UK by the promoters of stock transfer, who told council tenants they had a "unique opportunity" to improve their conditions or face further declines in services and investment.

Among the private companies seeking to profit from the redevelopment of Techwood and Clark Howell was none other than McCormack Baron Salazar (MBS), who went on to a similar operation in New Orleans. A variety of "options" were put to Atlanta tenants, with the usual empty promise of the "right to return". The reality is succinctly summarised by Lawrence Vale and Annemarie Gray:

> The case of the 1996 Olympics shows that a fortuitous mix of local, national and international factors could provide policy entrepreneurs the perfect conditions to support the kind of bold redevelopment they had dreamed about for decades. Purged of its poorest residents, the erstwhile Tech Flats/Techwood/Clark Howell Homes was once again a playing field for lucrative real estate ventures on the prime edge of downtown. Not until years later would the full extent of the displacement become clear. When the rental units of Centennial Place were all occupied, in 2000, only 78 families from the former Techwood and Clark Howell Homes were re-housed — just seven percent of the population when the planning process began.[157]

---

[157] "The Displacement Decathlon: Olympian struggles for affordable housing from Atlanta to Rio de Janeiro". *Placesjournal.org*, April 2013 .

Like their counterparts in other cities, the majority of displaced public housing tenants from Techwood and Clark Howell Homes were dispersed via housing choice vouchers. Centennial Place is the privatised mixed-income development of town houses that replaced their community and became part of the corporate landscape of central Atlanta where, in a grotesque juxtaposition, the Civil Rights Museum stands opposite Coca-Cola World!

After the Games are over

The Olympic Games only last a couple of weeks, but they reverberate for far longer. Mega-sports events, with their short-term popular and commercial appeal, act as Trojan Horses for speculative private property development. "Atlanta '96" helped pave the way for "London 2012" where a vast swathe of formerly public land, cleared and decontaminated at public expense, has become a building site for the private house building industry. Exploiting the marketing imagery of the London Games, the "East Village", with its own post/zip code ("E20"[158]), is a synthetic neighbourhood in Stratford buttressed by proximity to the Queen Elizabeth Park and massive Westfield shopping centre. The £500 million East Village scheme is being promoted by a partnership between two housing associations and First Base, a private development company which includes Blackstone among their investment partners. Half of the 2,800 new homes, converted from athletes' accommodation, are for market sale. The remaining 50 per cent have been split between "shared ownership", "affordable" private rent (up to 80 per cent of market levels) and "social" rent. Some say this represents a fitting part of the "legacy" for the £9.3 billion of public money spent on the Games. But it only reflects the pitiful rate of non-market homes produced elsewhere. The UK-based Bureau of Investigative Journalism found in 2013 that 60 per cent of new developments were

---

[158] In a strange twist of life imitating soap-opera, E20 was previously the postcode of Walford, the fictitious TV location of UK TV show East Enders.

falling short of local affordable housing targets, with developers repeatedly persuading local politicians and planners that doing more to meet housing need was "unviable".

In Atlanta, the 1996 Olympics became the catalyst for the virtual elimination of public housing, which had come to house a higher proportion of the city's population than any other US city. Centennial Place pioneered a different attitude to housing provision, combining income eligibility with a series of value judgments that exploited the stigmatisation of public housing and the people who lived in it. In what has become a macabre urban ritual, one of the last Atlanta Housing Authority developments, ironically named Roosevelt Homes,[159] was detonated on 27th February 2011. Since Pruitt-Igoe, the spectacle of public and council housing being blown-up has become a symbolic media staple. In a graphic UK illustration of the connection between neoliberal housing policy and corporate sports events, Glasgow city council had been planning to demolish its Red Road council flats as part of the opening ceremony of the 2014 Commonwealth Games![160]

Ball Pork

The use of sport as a vehicle for advancing the commercial conquest of the city extends beyond the four-year cycle of the Olympics and football/soccer World Cups. Building new stadiums as a mechanism for displacement, private housing and profiteering has occurred in many US cities, but nowhere more so than sport-fixated Atlanta. Using the precedent set by the 1996 Games, several sports franchises[161] in the city are in the process of developing new stadiums, a vital part of which is negotiating with local politicians for the most

---

[159] Another block named after Charles Palmer was pulled down at around the same time.
[160] Following an outcry, better sense prevailed and this idea was scrapped.
[161] It's important to note the differences between professional sports teams in the US and UK. In America, teams are treated as businesses that can be moved from place to place according to changing commercial circumstances. Most famously, this happened in 1957 when the Brooklyn Dodgers baseball club moved from New York City to Los Angeles, but has been repeated many times since.

advantageous and profitable use of public land and resources. The term "Ball Pork" was coined by Rob Herbert[162] as a pun on US "pork barrel" politics in which favours, prestige, patronage and public money are exchanged between politicians and business interests. This includes owners of sports teams who threaten to move to another city if they don't get what they want.

In a variation of and often alongside the arguments used to justify the destruction of public/council housing, perfectly good, serviceable and in some cases historic sports grounds are torn down to make way for more glamorous, corporately-branded stadiums, heavily subsidised by public money. A new stadium for the Atlanta Falcons[163] is being built adjacent to the 70,000 capacity Atlanta Dome which was only completed in 1992 with a $214 million subsidy from the Georgia General Assembly, but is now being dismantled. The Falcons' new venue (branded the Mercedes-Benz Stadium) was originally anticipated to cost local people an additional $200 million, but with the inevitable cost over-runs of the allegedly "efficient" private sector, is now expected to cost them $600 million, a significant proportion of the total budget. The clichéd justification is the completely unproven benefits of sports-led urban regeneration. In reality Atlanta is a prime example of the use of corporate sport and other mega-events to continue the reshaping of urban areas in a form that mirrors and exacerbates economic inequality.

A very similar phenomenon is in play at the 2012 Olympic Stadium near the "East Village" in Stratford, east London. With a total construction cost of £600 million, to which should be added the £1.8 billion value of transport and infrastructure improvements, from 2016 the stadium became the new home of West Ham United football club.[164] West Ham's wealthy owners are paying only £15

---

[162] "In America: Ball Pork", *New York Times*, 19th April 1998.
[163] An American Football team.
[164] Robbins G "From Upton Park to Olympic Park: What Does West Ham's Move Tell Us about Sport and Regeneration?", *Local Economy*, September 2015.

million towards the capital costs, in return for a 99-year lease at an annual rent of only £2 million. Part of the funding gap is being filled by a £40 million "loan" from the local authority, Newham Council, which represents one of the most impoverished areas in the UK and has a housing waiting list of over 20,000 families. Meanwhile West Ham's old ground has been sold to property developers who want to replace it with 838 new homes, none for non-market rent, an audacity challenged by a determined local campaign demanding 100 per cent genuinely affordable homes on a site in the heart of an ethnically-diverse working class community.[165]

The Atlanta vultures

The presence in Atlanta of the Blackstone Group and other property vultures emphasises the abandonment of the city's housing to global market forces. By the end of 2013, institutional investors were buying a quarter of homes for sale in the area, double the rate in 2010. As in Sacramento and across the US, corporate predators were feeding on the victims of the sub-prime foreclosure crisis. Previously family-owned homes were converted to "high end" rentals and used as collateral for further borrowing. Research by an Atlanta campaign group[166] found that tenants of Blackstone's "Invitation Homes" subsidiary faced higher rents, poor services, a remote or anonymous landlord, the constant fear of eviction and hidden fees that could increase their housing costs by 50 per cent – all things familiar to many private renters in the UK. The short-termism and unreliability of corporate private landlords was illustrated in July 2015 when Blackstone suddenly "dumped" 1,300 of its 8,600 Atlanta homes, amid speculation that the city's population was too impoverished to generate the kind of super-profits demanded by Blackstone's share-holders.

Another sign of the carving-up of central Atlanta are the numer-

---

[165] Campaigning has resulted in some improvement in the proposed scheme to allow for the usual modest and inadequate quota of non-market homes.

[166] "Blackstone: Atlanta's Newest Landlord", Occupy Our Homes Atlanta, April 2014.

ous hoardings bearing the logo of a global real estate investment company (with British roots) CBRE. A report by the company's Global Strategy and Research team sets out a list of reasons for increasing acquisition of sites in city centres.[167] These "urbanisation drivers" include the admission that developers adopt a strategy based on identifying "the path of least resistance" when negotiating with public authorities and appealing to "millennials" – people under 35 who "favour the convenience of urban-style environments". Like Blackstone, CBRE is increasing its portfolio of rented accommodation in Atlanta, which it describes as:

> ...one of the most popular cities to invest in at this time... More investors are seeking well-located Atlanta apartment communities than during the peak years of the last cycle. Opportunities are abundant for smart, aggressive capital.[168]

CBRE is also seeking to exploit the growth of private renting in the UK, which it estimates to be worth £500 billion. It has been involved in discussions with the British government aimed at removing "the barriers to institutional investment in private rented homes". CBRE's UK Head of Residential Research has commented:

> The Englishman's home may still be his [sic] castle, but increasingly he rents it rather than owns it. The UK population is expected to grow by 16 per cent over the next 25 years and this coupled with the declining affordability of home ownership means that demand for rental property is likely to remain strong. Current market conditions have created breathing space in the market to allow institutions to gain a foothold. There are a significant number of institutional investors actively considering the private rented sector and there have also been a number of private equity funds that have shown an interest...' [169]

---

[167] "US Urbanisation Trends: Investment implications for commercial real estate", CBRE, January 2015.

[168] "CBRE Global Investors Fund Acquires Atlanta Apartment Community", CBRE press release, 21st May 2013.

[169] CBRE company website, 17th August 2010.

Town and gown

Universities are another aggressive agency of urban restructuring and displacement in Atlanta. They have played a similar role in many other US and UK cities to the point where they've begun to closely resemble property development companies. Georgia Tech and Georgia State Universities (GSU) are embedded parts of the Atlanta political establishment and have substantial landholdings in the city. Since the Olympics nurtured the image of Atlanta as a "global city", the big universities have become steadily more powerful. This rise has dove-tailed with efforts to redesign Atlanta in accordance with its image as a symbol of the "New South". GSU development activity has dominated the downtown areas since the Olympics, after which they bought the athletes village, some of it on the site of the former Techwood/Clark Howell public housing, for $85 million. The rapid expansion plans of Atlanta's universities have consumed numerous other sites, including buildings whose historic and cultural importance hasn't saved them from the wrecking ball. In the early 1990s, GSU bought up and tore down a block that included Leb's Delicatessen, a place where the civil rights movement held early demonstrations against segregation.[170]

The marketisation of education mirrors that of housing and is a further sign of US and UK convergence. The principle of free access to higher education and the removal of financial barriers to working class students barely survived a generation in Britain. The same Labour government that systematically undermined council housing introduced student fees that inevitably created an American-style consumerist model in universities. This shift is reflected in ever-grander campuses designed to attract ever-more students, paying ever-higher fees. Simultaneously, as in US/UK housing policy, direct government funding to higher education has been dramatically cut, particularly since 2007/08. In response, like some

---

[170] For a chilling reminder of the racist climate of the time, see this interview with Leb's owner and staff from 1964: https://www.youtube.com/watch?v=6kNWqDcCrVs

housing providers, universities have become increasingly business-like and entrepreneurial.

University urban land-grabs aren't unique to Atlanta. One of many other US examples is Columbia University in New York City, which since the mid-2000s has been expanding north, gobbling up land that used to provide jobs and affordable homes to the local Harlem community. In the UK, although attempts of University College London to take over the Carpenters Estate next to the Olympic Park in Stratford were thwarted, the value of university expansion plans in London is estimated at £4 billion. Imperial College is developing a 25-acre scheme in White City, west London, partly on publically-owned land previously occupied by the BBC. Imperial's president (an American native) is explicit about the trans-Atlantic commercial links:

> I see London as becoming a university town that rivals Boston, with a financial centre that rivals New York, and an innovation and entrepreneurial environment that's growing up like San Francisco.[171]

Echoing the rhetoric of the benign property developer working for the common good, universities have been portrayed in some quarters as enlightened sculptors of the urban landscape, with their massive urban property deals a way of integrating academia with the community. An alternative interpretation sees universities as wealthy, powerful corporate institutions acting as agents of debt, displacement and gentrification.

Halls of residence

Student accommodation marks a critical inter-section between the international commercialised realms of education and housing. In the words of the property consultants Savills,[172] student accommo-dation has "evolved into a mature and globally recognised invest-

---

[171] "Overseas student surge drives expansion at London universities", *Financial Times*, 17th April 2015.

[172] "Spotlight UK Student Housing", Savills World Research 2015.

ment", worth £4.2 billion in the first five months of 2015 alone, 40 per cent above the previous peak in 2012. A profusion of purpose-built student housing is a feature of most UK cities and by far the most significant source of investment for it is the US. Some of the biggest North American corporate landlords, including Blackstone and Greystar, are particularly active in the sector. As well as the steady supply of students, some of them able to pay premium rates for housing, another appeal for developers is that student accommodation is sometimes considered part of their obligation to provide "affordable" housing. While public/council housing is denigrated for producing a "mono-culture", particularly if it's high-rise, skyscrapers of exclusively student housing are commonplace, like the 35-storey block Imperial College is planning at White City, backed by a REIT. But student accommodation and the commodification of education play a more insidious role. They are producing new generations of young people accustomed to debt and private renting, things the property industry thrives on.

Picking up the neoliberal pieces

As in Chicago, Atlanta's property development juggernaut has smashed a significant part of the city's social, as well as physical, infrastructure. Anita Beaty and Tim Franzen try to pick up the pieces. They also illustrate some of the changing features of organised opposition to big business-friendly housing policies. Anita has been a housing campaigner in Atlanta for 30 years and comes from a political tradition rooted in the civil rights, Cold War, anti-Vietnam war and counter-culture movements of the 1960s. Tim is a product of the anti-Iraq war, Occupy generation and a model of more fluid, reputedly less ideological, campaigning. They regard each other as comrades fighting the same enemy, with different styles and tactics.

The current centre of Anita Beaty's resistance is a former car dealership on Peachtree and Pine Streets that's now the downtown base of the Metro-Atlanta Taskforce for the Homeless. The Taskforce has been there since the Olympic year of 1996, when finding hostel accommodation for the homeless became a mainstream political priority. The 1920s art-deco building has obvious appeal to avaricious developers and has been valued at $9 million, but currently provides a bed for 500 homeless people a night. The city has a total of at least 12,000 homeless, of which 90 per cent are African-American, 40 per cent women and children. As a graphic indication of local housing demand, when the East Point municipality in south-west Atlanta advertised an allocation of housing vouchers in August 2010, over 30,000 people stood in a queue in 90 degrees heat just to get an application form. The ensuing chaos, with police in riot gear attempting to keep order, attracted national attention and provoked an NBC news broadcaster to ask "Aren't we better than this?"

Peachtree-Pine's high-profile central location is one reason why Anita Beaty has become a prime target for Atlanta's political establishment anxious to hide her activities and the reasons for them. Anita is particularly critical of the city's African-American politicians, some of whom were forged in the civil rights struggle but have become co-opted cheer-leaders for big business while trading on their past glories. Anita strongly associates this alliance with the destruction of Atlanta's public housing, which she directly links to the constant demand for the Peachtree shelter's services. She says:

> Thousands of perfectly good homes – and a community – became a wasteland. The Olympics gave the city to developers. They were our Katrina. We've become the poster-child for how not to do it by allowing a small group of individuals to take over. Now Atlanta's housing and urban policy *is* gentrification. They want a Disneyland Downtown and we have our hands full picking up the pieces.

Anita and her allies have fought an on-going battle with those seeking to close the hostel and move the homeless. The stigmatisation and criminalisation of Atlanta's poor and destitute was heralded in 1986 by an attempt to declare Peachtree Street a

Anita Beaty.

"Vagrant Free Zone", supported by former Mayor and Martin Luther King-associate Andrew Young.[173] Twenty-nine years later, Hackney Council in east London and several other UK public authorities attempted to introduce Public Space Protection Orders

---

[173] "Atlanta's vagrant fee zone stirs a protest", *New York Times*, 26th December 1986.

that would make "anti-social" behaviour like begging, sleeping rough or drinking alcohol illegal (and subject to a fine) in certain places.[174] Both Atlanta and Hackney authorities had to retreat in the face of opposition. But the underlying common theme – blaming the victims of failed housing policies – remains. The current Mayor of Atlanta, Kasim Reed, has vowed to close the Peachtree-Pine shelter, using Eminent Domain (the US equivalent of Compulsory Purchase) if necessary, and has even invoked a threat to the nation's health as justification for doing so, saying "it's one of the leading sites for tuberculosis in the nation...cases, not in Georgia, but across America, are being traced back to Peachtree... It has been tolerated for too long".[175]

Keeping the faith

In addition to varied political influences, Anita Beaty attributes some of her commitment to housing to her Christian Episcopalian faith. Tim Franzen runs the Atlanta Economic Justice Programme, an organisation funded by American Quakers. Religion is much nearer the surface of American housing campaigns than in the UK. It's not unusual for meetings and rallies to start with prayers and common for tenants to invoke religious belief as part of their motivation. This can contribute to an atmosphere akin to a revival meeting, with call and response, chanting and whooping far more common than in the more restrained climate of the UK. However, Tim's path to housing campaigning was shaped by what he describes as the "movement moment" of Occupy, which started in New York's Wall Street in September 2011 but spawned numerous imitations around the US and has significantly influenced the direction of opposition politics in the country. As Tim recalls:

---

[174] "PSPOs: The new control orders threatening our public spaces", *The Guardian*, 8th September 2015.
[175] "Mayor Reed wants to shutter Peachtree and Pine homeless facility, build new one", *Atlanta Business Chronicle*, 11th August 2015.

There was this great, creative, exciting, bold thing happening that was opening up a conversation around wealth inequality that hadn't happened in my lifetime. It changed the national lexicon. Talking about "The 1%" has become normal.

Tim is critical of the failure of some on the political left to constructively engage with Occupy. He estimates there are between 40,000 and 50,000 full-time, paid political organisers in the US, an astonishing figure by UK standards. But Tim says too many operate in "issue silos", are compromised by their funding sources or only want to "write articles". But he argues that Occupy did not present a sustainable, winnable strategy, partly because it failed to engage a sufficiently broad coalition around the daily-life issues confronting working class communities. Like thousands of other Atlantans, Tim experienced these issues first-hand during the foreclosure crisis. He was the first person from his family to buy a home, with a loan to cover the purchase price of $89,000. The house had risen in price a few years later to $150,000 but plunged to $30,000 when the subprime storm hit. Like so many others, the money Tim had invested and accumulated in his Atlanta home was wiped out as the result of actions that originated on Wall Street. Keeping people in their homes, while stopping banks from taking them over, has became the practical focus of housing campaigns in Atlanta and a way of harnessing and extending the energy of the Occupy movement. As Tim recalls:

> We wanted to win stuff for ordinary, everyday people and foreclosure was really hurting the city. We don't have any public housing left, so homeownership became a priority because it had become the priority for many low-income people in Atlanta. African-American communities were ravaged by subprime. People who'd put all their pennies into their home lost it. Some neighbourhoods like Peoplestown and Mechanicsville are littered with abandoned homes. So we started working around individual campaigns to keep individuals in their homes and use that as a springboard for organising in the neighbourhood.

The tactics used recaptured the spirit of the city's civil rights movement – sit-ins at banks, encampments and blockades to stop threatened evictions – and succeeded in saving several dozen families from homelessness. Now the focus has shifted. The activities of global corporate landlords and the conversion of thousands of homes from owner-occupation to renting means building a tenant movement is Tim's new priority. The focal point is yet another of the city's sports stadiums. The Turner Field Community Benefits Coalition is an alliance of civil society organisations, including churches, charities and cross-tenure resident groups, demanding the planned redevelopment of the former Olympic stadium, built on 77 acres of public land, genuinely benefit the local community. The redevelopment is led by the omnipresent Georgia State University who, incredibly, want to replace the existing stadium with two new ones. Local campaigners want a transparent development process and at least 30 per cent affordable housing based on "our definition of affordable, not theirs". Hundreds of tenants are involved, but Tim Franzen acknowledges: "There's a long way to go. Big property is an adversary that seems impossible to beat, but when we organise smart, we have the capacity to win. We don't know our own strength".[176]

Philanthropic funding

Atlanta's combination of old money and relatively progressive politics creates a particular dynamic around a general issue that faces many housing campaigns – philanthropic funding. Finding the money to support political activity that may challenge the status quo is a perennial problem, particularly in the context of shrinking public finance. In the absence of mainstream grants, campaign organisations increasingly look to private, corporate and charitable trusts and foundations to support their activities. This is more

---

[176] In April 2017, residents erected a tent city at the gates of Turner Field as part of their on-going campaign. For more details see www.turnerfieldcoalition.org

prevalent in the US, but is becoming common in the UK too. A difficult balance is often needed between pragmatically accepting
money for work that may not otherwise happen and being compromised or constricted by the source of that money. This dilemma is
further complicated by the role of non-profit, third sector organisations, of which there are many in Atlanta. Some are funded by
Coca-Cola's Woodruff Foundation or the Cousins Foundation,
owned by a property development company directly involved in the
destruction of the city's public housing. The role of non-profits is
pointedly questioned by the Atlanta Progressive News website:

> How is it that in Atlanta, Georgia, the birthplace of the Civil Rights
> Movement, the powers of corporate wealth and the bourgeoisie have
> managed to destroy public housing, decimate low-income communi-
> ties, privatise public schools, privatise Grady Hospital, enact draco-
> nian anti-panhandling legislation, and carry out a war upon
> low-income people, despite the presence of so many non-profit organ-
> isations and other advocacy organisations that purport to speak on
> behalf of low-income people?[177]

This litany of privatisation is familiar from New Orleans and
illustrates both the all-consuming scope of the neoliberal project –
with or without hurricanes – and the failure of the non-profit establishment to consistently oppose it. Both the US and UK have examples of the high-profile collapse of campaign organisations that
became dependent on what, at least in retrospect, were unsustainable and potentially compromising sources of philanthropic and
corporate finance. Ultimately, as both Anita Beaty and Tim Franzen
argue, only autonomous self-organisation and funding from
accountable public sources or trade unions can protect important
campaigns and services from the wavering fortunes and tastes of
the non-profit industrial complex.

---

[177] "Race, Poverty and Non-Profits in Atlanta, a devastating critique",
atlantaprogressivenews.com 13th June 2013.

Conclusion

Despite its unique history, Atlanta can be seen as the paradigm of the US city. The transition from post-agrarian to rapidly industrialising, densely populated metropolis inter-cut with ethnic and class tension, gave way to post-war suburban sprawl that re-inscribed skin colour on the housing landscape. Public housing, which mirrored all these developments, eventually became the target for the corporate recapture of the central city. The glamour zone of the central business district attempts to conceal the social flux at the heart of Atlanta. The make-over of working class urban neighbourhoods is accompanied by reverse segregation, as African-American Atlantans are pushed towards the social and physical isolation of the city's suburban fringe where, according to the Brookings Institute, the poverty rate increased by 159 per cent between 2000 and 2011.[178]

Atlanta's urban experience should be set alongside the special circumstances of the South, a region that continues to influence the political culture of the country as a whole. The unresolved tensions of racism, discrimination and inequality continue to simmer and occasionally boil over. On 17th June 2015, I was standing outside the Ebenezer Baptist Church in the area just east of downtown Atlanta, where Martin Luther King Jr was born, raised and worshipped. At the same time, in another church 300 miles away in Charleston, South Carolina nine black people were murdered by a white-supremacist with a fixation for the old Confederacy flag. In the days afterwards, a national debate raged about the legitimacy of flying "the stars and bars" and some Southern states took the belated decision to stop doing so. The assertion that "Black Lives Matter" continues to define a campaign that rivals the Occupy movement in its ability to trouble the conscience of the nation.

Some housing campaigners have added Black Homes Matter to their slogans and nowhere is this more true than Atlanta, with an

---

[178] "Suburbs and the new American poverty", *The Atlantic*, 7th January 2015.

additional resonance born of the city's distinctive political culture described by Anita Beaty as "A lot of Southern Good Ol' Boys and Girls, where everyone's polite while they take your housing from under you". Tim Franzen adds: "Whatever problems there are in America are magnified in the South".

Atlanta exemplifies the wish-fulfilment of contemporary US and UK housing and urban policy. Working class neighbourhoods have been razed and replaced with zones of consumption and exchange populated by affluent urbanites. Public housing and other public services have been destroyed and a new generation of the dispossessed has been removed to the hinterland.

8

Washington DC: The belly of the beast

Introduction

My US housing journey ended in the place where the policies that shape the lives of 300 million Americans and an untold number of non-Americans begin. In 1989, UK economist John Williamson listed ten criteria that formed what he called "The Washington Consensus": a set of objectives that could advance the cause of neoliberalism on a global scale, including privatisation, deregulation and the promotion of private property rights. In essence, these are now the ideological precepts that inform housing policies at the local level in many places throughout the US and UK. They are lobbied for, crafted and disseminated in a city with an identity that is physically monumental, socially polarised and politically byzantine on a scale rivalled only by the Vatican.

Nor is Washington DC immune to the housing problems that issue from its midst. On the contrary, the city or "District" features many of the dynamics of privilege and exclusion found elsewhere, though its contradictions are rarely exposed beneath the veneer of its public image.

It's important to understand something of DC's special history and character.[179] The capital, like the country, is relatively young, consecrated for its administrative purpose in 1800. The hope was that the new planned city could straddle the North-South economic and political divide. Its geographic neutrality is enshrined in the US Constitution, which makes DC a protectorate of the Federal government, thus "owned" by the democratic apparatus of the people. DC is a company town in the business of government. But its 650,000 residents are constitutionally denied direct representation at the national level and local politics is often over-shadowed by the mechanics of Federal power.[180] DC's unusual personality is reinforced by its physicality. The District is

---

[179] Bordewich F (2008) *Washington: The making of the American Capital*, New York, Harper Collins.

[180] The District of Columbia is not a state, so not represented in Congress. This issue is regularly the subject of campaigns for reform.

legally constrained within a ten by ten mile diamond from which the state of Virginia, in 1848, took a bite from the south-west corner. During the Civil War, which socially and demographically transformed the city, it was surrounded by fortifications and the sense, if not the reality, of a walled city remains, albeit in an increasingly significant relationship with its porous and increasingly poor suburbs.

The popular media image of DC as a seat of State belies its many other qualities, not least as one of America's first cities with a majority African-American population who nicknamed it "Chocolate City". DC was segregated until the mid-1950s. The Shaw/U Street district, barely a mile north of the White House, became a centre of black economic poverty alongside cultural richness to rival Harlem.[181] The city remains strongly defined by geographic location, in part because of its layout (a variation on the grid system): divided into quadrants with cross-cutting indexed streets and avenues that are a legacy of the original plan to create a grand capital to rival those of Europe. This splendour is reflected in the opulent homes in quiet, tree-lined streets of some neighbourhoods. But this genuinely compact city is one of sharp contrasts, where wealth may be just around the corner from poverty. DC's historic heterogeneity is now seriously threatened by housing policies that are pushing the poor and black out, while sucking the rich and white in.

Near South East

The "Near South East" area exemplifies what's happening in DC and the US, with the additional significance that it's taking place a 20-minute walk from the domed Capitol building. Visiting in 2015, it's impossible to visualise what it looked like two decades earlier. Today, Near South East has been rebranded Capitol Riverfront, an artificial marketing label designed to conceal the fact that, 20 years earlier, the area was dominated by the Arthur Capper/Carrollsburg

---

[181] Ruble B A (2012) *Washington's U Street: A biography*, Washington DC, Woodrow Wilson Centre Press.

public housing development.[182] In place of 700 affordable rented homes, local shops, workshops and a tight-knit community, are now thousands of private apartments, hotels, bars and restaurants. Arthur Capper/Carrollsburg was emptied and demolished in the mid-2000s, with two of the usual suspects at the controls – HOPE VI and a sports stadium. The latter is Nationals Park, which landed in the area as the new home of the city's baseball team, financed with a public dowry of $700 million ($260 more than the original estimate). Like their Atlanta counterparts, DC politicians and developers remain addicted to Ball Pork and are currently planning another stadium in the adjacent South West district, again financed with apparently limitless public money.

Rose Oliphant remembers Capper/Carrollsburg as "beautiful": a place where people looked after each other, even in cash-tight, drug-blighted and sometimes violent circumstances. Now she says "it doesn't feel like a neighbourhood any more". This is how the redevelopment agency describes what replaced it:

> ...a growing district-within-the-District that extends the city's skyline to the water's edge... Located just five blocks south of the US Capitol building, the Front offers the best in city living with the extraordinary advantages of a riverfront setting, a distinct maritime and industrial heritage and *access to what matters*...[183]

"What matters" has renamed the area, obliterated the memory of Capper/Carrollsburg and replaced it with 3,200 private apartments, 7.3 million square feet of office space, 27 restaurants, a private gym and a pet store. This is only a fraction of the developers' ambition for an area described, with approval, by the Urban Land Institute as experiencing "one of the fastest transformations of an urban neighbourhood in the US". A frenzy of activity is seeing

---

[182] A 2007 documentary, *Chocolate City* by Sam Wild and Ellie Walton, poignantly captures the social trauma of Capper/Carrollsburg's destruction in the context of DC's surge of private property development.

[183] Capitol Riverfront Business Improvement District Annual Report 2009, my emphasis.

"developers jumping in with two feet"[184] in an effort to attract the fabled population of "millennials" they see as guarantors of the affluent 21st century city.

Rose Oliphant is one of the few former public housing tenants who managed to return to the area after redevelopment. Her friends and neighbours have been scattered to other parts of the city and region, particularly the once-marginalised but now gentrifying Anacostia district across the river of the same name. As ever, the empty "right to return" promise was made by the authorities, but for most it was not kept. Local playwright Anu Yadev, whose play *Capers* describes the destruction of the Capper/Carrollsburg community, says this was never the intention: "It was about remapping cities so that poor people don't live there anymore. Only middle class poor people are allowed to return".

The changes Rose has experienced have led her to question her sense of belonging and place in Washington DC:

> The future of DC is tearing down and building up, but there won't be any more public housing. There'll be more homeless people… The culture of black people, the places we used to be able to afford to live, are being destroyed. But it's not about colour. It's about money.

Links in the developer's chain

Capitol Riverfront is yet another example of the identikit remodelling of former industrial waterfront areas from Seattle to Salford, Baltimore to Birmingham and Washington DC to London. There is now a trans-Atlantic freemasonry of self-defined "experts" and "place makers" who claim special knowledge of how to revitalise what they portray as redundant wastelands. In fact, these were often places where people lived and worked, with an identity that pre-dates the ahistorical presumptions of commercial marketing strategies.

---

[184] "Former D.C. planner Andy Altman returns to a neighbourhood he dreamed up", *Washington Post*, 23rd January 2015.

One of the DC planners credited with drawing the blueprint for Capitol Riverfront had his next job in London, overseeing the yet-to-be delivered "legacy" of the 2012 Olympics. Returning to the US, he joined the board of directors of a "non-profit real estate developer". As though this were not sufficient oxymoron, the company, called The Community Builders (TCB), describes itself as being in "the community development industry". TCB captures the ambiguities of the contemporary housing world in which the lines between commercial and non-commercial activities are increasingly – and deliberately – blurred. In its early days, TCB played a leading role in the development of Tent City in Boston, an important victory for housing justice campaigners in the city (see p 18, 21). Among its recent projects are ownership or management of 11,000 homes, involvement in HUD's Choice Neighbourhoods Initiative and the redevelopment and de facto privatisation of public housing. Despite claims of altruism, several of the company's directors have links to private developers and finance companies.

TCB are part of a distinctively American approach to urban policy with ominous portents for the UK. The tradition of charitable services for the poor pioneered by the likes of Jane Adams in Chicago failed to solve enduring poverty and discrimination, reflected in numerous urban uprisings, particularly during the 1960s. In 1966, Bobby Kennedy sponsored the formation of Community Development Corporations (CDCs) as independent, privately-operated agencies operating at local level with a combination of private and public finance. Senator Daniel Patrick Moynihan, who interpreted urban inequality in explicitly racialised terms, described CDCs as an attempt to "get the market to do what the bureaucracy cannot". Property developers were at the forefront of this initiative. The archetypal benevolent real estate magnate of the period was James Rouse. Based in Washington DC, Rouse got involved in a housing renovation project led by members of the church where he worshipped in the Adams Morgan area of the city (subsequently rapidly gentrified). Rouse, who died in 1996, went on to build an entire new city, Columbia in Maryland, about 30 miles north east of DC, based on his characteristically American combination of utopian and commercial motives. But his Rouse Corporation also undertook gargantuan property deals like Harborplace in Baltimore, which has direct conceptual and financial links to the redevelopment of Brindleyplace in Birmingham, England.

In 1982, Rouse founded the Enterprise Foundation (now known as Enterprise Community Partners), which exploited the introduction in 1986 of Low Income Housing Tax Credits (LIHTCs) channelling billions of dollars into forms of "affordable" housing. LIHTCs have become the US government's primary policy tool for providing non-market housing. They provide tax-breaks and indirect public subsidies via front organisations for private developers hostile to direct provision of public housing. Enterprise Community Partners (ECP) describes its core business as "syndicating tax credit equity investments" to finance sub-market housing. Its trustees feature the expected collection of real estate and banking executives, including Tony Salazar of MBS, leading exponents of public housing elimination. LIHTCs, which some are touting in the UK, have helped finance 2.4 million homes in the US, but as Enterprise Community Partners itself admits, has failed to meet the scale of the country's housing need:

> The US is in the midst of a housing insecurity crisis that affects nearly 19 million low-income families. The crisis touches families who are homeless or pay more than half their monthly income on housing. They struggle to stay afloat and face impossible choices – such as choosing to pay rent or buy groceries. Many families are one paycheck away from losing their homes. Tomorrow, they might be on the street.[185]

---

[185] ECP website, www.enterprisecommunity.org

Aping the non-profit, corporate model

The CDC and LIHTC models raise critical issues for current and future housing policy in the UK. The origins, development and trajectory of US CDCs closely resemble those of the UK housing association movement: from philanthropy, through acting as a business and government-friendly alternative to direct public investment, before adopting a commercial culture, albeit one disguised with claims of social conscience. The US experience presents a very clear evidence-based housing policy choice – direct and accountable government investment, or indirect (but still largely government funded) investment controlled by a clique of corporate vested interests?

Another fundamental question flows from the CDC model, with implications beyond housing: how credible is "community building" carried out by external non-profit agencies receiving a cocktail of finance, including public funding, but often with close links to the private sector? The concept of "community" has become a centre-piece of UK urban policy.[186] Much of the impetus for this approach derives from US initiatives founded on the perception of urban problems as essentially pathological and rooted in the "chaotic" or "dysfunctional" lifestyles of the "underclass". Such language has become so commonplace in the UK that it's hard to recall that it's a relatively recent US import, albeit one based on a longer tradition of Victorian paternalism. The 21st century re-introduction of a 19th century lexicon of judgementalism was explicitly signalled by UK prime minister Tony Blair in 2002. With direct reference to the US experience, Blair twinned "rights and responsibilities" in New Labour's flagship New Deal for Communities programme, a classic example of what A H Halsey described as "ideas drifting casually across the Atlantic, soggy on arrival and of dubious utility".[187]

---

[186] Cochrane A (2007) *Understanding Urban Policy: A critical approach*, Oxford, Blackwell Publishing.
[187] *Times Educational Supplement*, 9th February 1973.

Museum Square

Like other US cities, Washington DC suffered a post-war population haemorrhage. The Southeast Freeway that traverses the District was part of DC's 1950/60s urban renewal programme. It became known as "white flight freeway" as it opened the route to the suburbs over the wreckage of African-American neighbourhoods. The aim of repopulating the city has been intrinsic to justifying the private property development mania now gripping DC. One of the latest targets is the largely Chinese community of low-income housing tenants who live at Museum Square in the central Mount Vernon Triangle area of the city. In June 2014, the private owners of the 300-home complex, the ominously named Bush Corporation, announced they wanted to demolish it and replace scarce sub-market housing with 800 private luxury apartments. In another astonishing example of brazen, callous profiteering, the company's spokesperson said:

> We're trying to maximise the value of the property. We've had the building there for 30-plus years and we think the building has run its course of usefulness. And everyone who lives there is getting vouchers so we don't think of it as displacement.[188]

For those 30 years, the owners have received huge government subsidies in the form of the vouchers their low-income tenants needed to pay the rent. But now Bush Corp. want to cash in on the extra profits on offer in an area where the median monthly rent for a one bedroom flat is $2,350. Their "expiring lease" with HUD would displace some of the last remaining Chinese residents of central DC, but Museum Square residents aren't going without a fight. After a lively, well-attended demonstration on 23rd June 2015, supported by the National Alliance of HUD Tenants (NAHT) and other DC housing rights campaigners, Jiaxin Lin, aged 10,

---

[188] "Black, Asian residents unite to save low-income building near Chinatown", *Washington Post*, 6th August 2014.

summed up the iniquity of the housing crisis with the piercing simplicity of a child:

> The owner wants us to move and build a building for the rich people. It's not fair for the people who live here. Some people are afraid and want to move quickly, but then we won't be able to stand up and fight. This demonstration shows how people feel and that we're working really hard to save our homes.[189]

Project-Based Section 8

The situation at Museum Square is indicative of a national trend posing another serious threat to non-market rented housing in the US. It demonstrates again that the private sector is an unreliable friend in meeting housing need and that indirect forms of State funding for housing are counterproductive and unsustainable. Jiaxin Lin's home was built under a programme established by HUD in 1974. Project-Based Section 8 gave tax incentives to developers to build apartment blocks and in return tied them into a 30-year agreement to accept low-income tenants unable to afford the full market rent. 1.3 million homes were provided under the scheme, with qualifying tenants paying 30 per cent of their income on rent and the government paying an additional top-up to the landlord, a subsidy that averages $700 per home, per month and costs the government a total of $9.7 billion a year. Many of these agreements are now ending, as at Museum Square. Since 1995, about 360,000 Project Based Section 8 homes have been lost as private developers, having reaped the rewards of tax-breaks and guaranteed rent underwritten by the Federal government, seek to cash in on even higher profits by converting to full market rents.

---

[189] NAHT supported another demonstration at Museum Square a year later, which I also attended. The fight to save Museum Square continues, but as Jiaxin Lin feared, some tenants have moved out. Options for a possible tenant buy-out of the building are being explored. See "Here Until They Take Me Out: DC tenants use the law to fight gentrification", *The Guardian*, 3rd January 2017.

Another 450,000 affordable homes are currently threatened by these expiring leases. Many of the households facing an uncertain future have a family member who is elderly or disabled.

Project-Based Section 8 is just one of a number of complicated funding mechanisms that make up America's subsidised low-income housing picture. It is a system so complex that it's hard to avoid the conclusion it's designed to deter people from entering it in the first place, or from understanding and challenging it if they do. This convoluted, bureaucratic maze imposes additional strains on housing campaigners who face a constant challenge to navigate and interpret it without becoming sucked into a legalistic quagmire. It has an additional effect of distancing tenants from the source of the political decisions that determine their housing fates, compounding a danger of resignation to forces that seem beyond their control. Above all however, indirect forms of housing subsidy, like Housing Benefit in the UK (currently costing the government £25 billion a year), disguise the fundamental problem of a housing system unable to meet the needs of millions of people without enriching private landlords with huge amounts of public money that could otherwise be invested in permanent, affordable homes.

Greenbelt

An alternative to housing based on the caprice of the market and individualism can be found just outside Washington DC. Greenbelt, now a town with a population of 24,000, was originally part of a bold, but ultimately thwarted, programme to build homes through direct government investment and a model of publicly-owned housing built on publicly owned land. Like other State-led housing initiatives, Greenbelt emerged from crisis. Along with a myriad of infrastructure projects, the New Deal used house building as a stimulus to the shattered economy of the Great Depression. President Roosevelt's planning advisor, Rexford Tugwell, envisioned 3,000 new towns across the US, inspired by the UK Garden Cities model. The plan was immediately accused of being "socialistic" and

Greenbelt Cinema.

dramatically whittled down to three,[190] of which Greenbelt is the largest. Like Ebenezer Howard (p32-33), Clarence Stein (p33) and the Levitts (p42), Tugwell believed the answer to urban congestion and squalor was to escape the city and start again in the countryside with a comprehensive vision of physical and social planning. Greenbelt's first 885 low-density homes, for which there were 5,700 applicants, were intended for married couples with modest incomes. The new homes were clustered in pedestrian-only zones with Radburn-like walkways linking local shops and amenities in an environment of woods and lakes. The first families (all white)[191] arrived in 1937 and as well as meeting financial criteria, had to express a willingness to support community activities.

---

[190] In addition to Greenbelt, Greenhills (Ohio) and Greendale (Wisconsin).
[191] Today, 40 per cent of Greenbelt residents are African-American.

Like Letchworth in the UK and Rochdale Village in New York City, Greenbelt nurtured a range of cooperative institutions. The town's centrepiece is the Roosevelt Centre, a collection of sleek, flat-roofed, white buildings including the New Deal cafe, supermarket, credit union and cinema, all still run as co-operatives. Nearby are two public swimming pools, a library and a community centre adorned with friezes that celebrate the early idealism of the town and nation. The community's founding spirit was reaffirmed in 1952 when the government wanted to privatise Greenbelt and residents formed a cooperative that acquired – and continues to own and manage – the original 1,600 homes.

Judith Davis, Greenbelt's former Mayor, sits amid the town's splendid Art Deco civic architecture and reflects on being a resident for 40 years and a long-time member of the residents elected governing council. She feels the town retains its special identity, but is acutely aware of the difficulties in preserving an island of public-spirited municipalism in a sea of private isolationism, sprawling development and market excess.

> It's much more ethnically diverse and that's good: it's more lively. Every night there's something going on, at least here in the town centre. But it's hard. A lot of people today don't understand the cooperative system. We also have sky-rocketing prices and rents for the new homes in the area.

Some of Greenbelt's original 1930s residents still live there. Judith feels the communal spirit is increasingly dependent on this older generation and jeopardised by the absence of a decent local public transport system and growing market-driven transience in the private rented sector. She also draws attention to an issue of mounting importance for trans-Atlantic housing policy: the linkage between a persons' housing situation and their quality of life in retirement and old age. In Judith's words, the co-operative renters of Greenbelt "hang on for as long as they can", paying an affordable rent, but in a place without specialist care for the elderly. In a country with a marketised healthcare system, those without big pensions, savings or significant equity in their home can find themselves quickly reduced to penury by medical costs or fluctuations in the housing market.

The area around the original idealistic Greenbelt settlement now has the familiar look of car-oriented suburban tracts, shopping malls, sterile commercial developments and congested highways. This is exacerbated by an influx of people driven out of DC by rising housing costs. Greenbelt is in Prince George's County, a jurisdiction that between 2000 and 2010 saw its Hispanic population double, its black population increase by 10 per cent and the number of white residents fall by 34 per cent. During this period, average incomes in the area remained flat, another example of the creeping impoverishment of the suburbs that were once the symbol of American affluence and aspiration.[192]

Greenbelt is another reminder of American utopianism and a striking relic of an enlightened but fleeting period in US housing and public policy. A new wave of private property speculation could further detach Greenbelt from its origins if, as is possible, the FBI relocates there. This would be a strange irony given that organisation's historic hostility to the ideals Greenbelt represents. Nonetheless, the impulse to build new places from scratch remains deeply imbedded in US and UK urban policy making which, as David Harvey observes, have a history "fraught with utopian dreams".[193] Successive UK governments have sought to recapture the achievements of the post-war New Towns that ultimately provided homes for 2.7 million people in 32 settlements, a programme on a scale that approached Rexford Tugwell's New Deal ambitions. But what current New Town and Eco-Town advocates, including the UK government, fail to recognise is that the previous success of such policies was founded on removing housing from the tyranny of the

---

[192] "Changes in Prince George's County: 2000 through 2010", The Urban Institute, December 2011.

[193] Harvey D (2000) *Spaces of Hope*, Edinburgh, Edinburgh University Press.

market and thus ensuring a stable context for long term planning and investment in the public interest. The healthy 79 year-old heart of Greenbelt demonstrates the lasting benefits of this approach in comparison to the degenerating body of free-market excess swirling around it.

NAHT

The organisation Charlotte Delgado from Sacramento (p134) has given so much of her energy to holds its annual conference in Washington DC in June. The National Alliance of HUD Tenants (NAHT) faces logistical, as well as political, challenges that dwarf those of its UK counterparts. Co-ordinating an organisation across thousands of miles and several time zones makes significant demands on a membership that is almost entirely composed of low-income tenants living in places that may have very little in common other than a shared battle to save their homes. The multitude of ways in which affordable housing is under attack is collected in the vivid testimonies of the people who come to NAHT conference. Speakers tell local tales of battles with giant corporate landlords, sleazy private slumlords, disinterested politicians and labyrinthine bureaucracy, and relate them to the chronic injustice of national government policy. A harder political edge has developed at NAHT conference over the years and assumed additional impetus after the 2003 invasion of Iraq, 2007 market crash and 2011 Occupy movement. There are now constant references to the disparity between State spending on war, the bank bailouts, tax breaks for the 1% and affordable homes. But NAHT members also increasingly link distorted US housing policy to a wider set of social issues, particularly low pay, healthcare, education, police brutality and racism. There was a moment, in 2008, when a sense of optimism spread through NAHT conference at the prospect of a Barack Obama victory, but a year later one delegate rhetorically asked of the new president "OK, you're black. What else have you got?"

Despite such scepticism, almost all NAHT members who declare a party political affiliation are Democrats, but the limitations of the two-party duopoly are raised repeatedly and reflected in the voter apathy that NAHT is anxious to confront. Given its poor, non-home-owning and often African-American, disabled and elderly demographic, there is acute awareness that NAHT members are among the groups who may not participate in elections. Conference delegates are implored to vote themselves and encourage others to do so. But the chronic levels of election non-participation among working class Americans remains a pivotal element in the marginalisation of NAHT members and the causes they stand for.

Overseeing, co-ordinating and shaping NAHT's activities is its executive director, Michael Kane – another unsung American hero and like Charlotte Delgado in California and Anita Beaty in Georgia, a "late blooming hippy" with long roots in the US progressive movement. Originally from Texas, since the early 1970s Michael has lived in Boston, where NAHT has its national office. He was involved in the successful Tent City campaign alongside Mel King (p18) and has acquired a vast knowledge of the US housing struggles to which he has dedicated his life. Over the years, Michael has been instrumental in saving hundreds, possibly thousands, of affordable homes across the US, through a judicious combination of political alliance building, lobbying and action, both inside and outside the political mainstream. While he has never sought personal reward – material or otherwise – for his vocation, Michael also personifies the perennial dilemma of the driven campaigner who assumes a role that is politically, personally and medically unsustainable. The question of "leadership succession" is one that NAHT, like many similar campaigns, finds difficult to resolve.

The Progressive Caucus

Michael Kane is linked to another, often concealed, feature of the American political scene. The common assumption is that US electoral politics is defined and dominated by a narrow band of opinion around an essentially right-wing agenda. While the

Michael Kane.

Republican/Democrat grip on national power is inherently conservative, with some politicians espousing reactionary views that would be unlikely to be expressed so openly in the UK, there are also far more politicians who might be described as "left wing" than is usually recognised. Terminology becomes tricky in this arena because, notwithstanding Bernie Sanders and a few others, there is still a stigma around the term "socialist", and its milder alternative "liberal" can also be politically toxic. It's perhaps for this reason that a group of politicians elected to the US Congress have described themselves as The Congressional Progressive Caucus (CPC).

The CPC was established in 1991 and in 2015 had 75 members from the House of Representatives and one from the Senate, Bernie

Sanders. While much of the CPC's activities might be confined to the "Inside the Beltway" world of Washington DC politics, its policies also connect with a tide of radicalism in the country as a whole that is demanding a change to the status quo. The clearest example of this is The People's Budget, a $1.9 trillion manifesto that speaks directly to the growing inequality in America and seeks to revive the nation's longer tradition of progressive politics. Alongside calls for public investment in infrastructure, job creation and extension of workers' rights, the CPC demand higher taxes on wealthy companies and individuals, reductions in military spending and an end to the "sequestration" or budget cuts that have damaged affordable housing so much since 2007. Although in somewhat vague terms, the CPC also acknowledges the housing crisis by calling for a fully-funded programme to make a home "affordable and accessible for all Americans". Taken as a whole, the CPC platform is at least on a par with the rhetoric of the Corbyn UK Labour Party and it is highly unlikely that 75 British MPs would put their names to such policies. However, the extraordinary popularity of campaigns led by Sanders and Corbyn (and in a perverse way, those of Donald Trump and Nigel Farage too) indicate that the Washington Consensus may have cracked in the US and UK.

In the aftermath of the November 2016 Presidential election, the CPC said "Donald Trump's campaign was built on insulting and scapegoating immigrants, women, and ethnic and religious minorities". It remains embroiled in challenging President Trump's legislative agenda and promoting a new People's Budget based on opposing austerity and on "a brighter future for all Americans". These slogans chimed with the huge anti-Trump demonstrations on the streets of the US, UK and around the world following his inauguration.

Conclusions

The complacent claim by the Bush Corporation that when Museum Square residents are evicted "we don't think of it as displacement" marks a vital dividing line in current US/UK housing policy. Some

NAHT members.

politicians, academics and policy-makers share the Bush Corp. view that forms of non-market housing are inter-changeable, along with the people who live in it. They argue that, so long as alternative accommodation is provided, possibly with equivalent public subsidy, the consequences of removing people from their homes are mitigated. Thus the provision of Section 8 vouchers in the US, or Housing Benefit payments in the UK, even if they necessitate tenants moving to other parts of the city or beyond it, are treated as benign. But family, kinship and community networks are not transplantable, particularly for working class people for whom sources of mutual support and identity can be crucial. These are qualities that can't always be reduced to monetary terms, but when housing policy is dominated by corporate commercial interests, it's blind to deeper social, human values. Tent City in Boston, the Amalgamated Co-Op in the Bronx, Greenbelt, Maryland and the best examples of public housing in the US and UK show how things can be done differently, by creating an alternative to the tyranny of the market.

For now, the policies from "The Hill" in Washington DC are horribly skewed towards the dog eat dog short-termism of the housing market. This is founded on hypocrisy. The myth that private home-ownership is a mark of independent financial self-sufficiency, while non-market renting represents State dependency, is exposed by Richard Florida who describes "the real problem with American housing policy".[194] According to Professor Florida, each year the US government spends four times as much on subsidies to "wealthy and middle class home owners" as it does on affordable housing for its poorest citizens (even based on the most generous interpretation of "affordable", including vouchers and Low Income Housing Tax Credits). This gross distortion of housing priorities is now replicated in the UK and given added momentum by the Housing and Planning Act which seeks to replace government investment in non-market rented housing with subsidies for private home ownership. Former chief executive of the UK's Chartered Institute of Housing John Perry writes:

> ...out of total housing investment of over £44bn between now and 2020, only about £2bn will now go to sub-market rented housing. Another, bigger part of the budget will go to Starter Homes and shared ownership housing – some £6.4bn. All of the rest, whether grants, loans or guarantees, is directed at helping first-time buyers or otherwise stimulating the private market. [195]

---

[194] 'The US spends far more on homeowner subsidies that it does on affordable housing', *CityLab*, 17th April 2015.
[195] "Poor Relation", *Inside Housing*, 11th July 2016. NB: These figures have changed slightly since. See "UK Housing Review 2016 Briefing Paper", (p11) Chartered Institute of Housing.

Conclusion – A cautionary tale and a call for action

At the end of his 1937 tour of the US, Richard Reiss concluded that, while there was no "one sovereign cure to the evils of bad housing", there was no solution without "public housing and substantial financial assistance from the Federal government". Eighty years later, the same holds true. But the complexity and severity of the 21st century trans-Atlantic housing crisis can't be solved with 20th century measures. My 2015 US journey chronicles the many social consequences of an economic system with speculative property investment disastrously enmeshed within it. Untangling it requires a fundamental reappraisal of how we treat housing in our society and an honest assessment of what has – and has not – worked in the past.

Having a significant proportion of homes removed from the market nexus is an essential, but not sufficient, step towards a more stable, equitable housing policy. The exact form of how this is done should be subject to genuine local democratic debate. But this requires unwinding the welter of social and moral judgments that increasingly accompany perceptions of different forms of housing. The aspiration for private home ownership need not be the enemy of non-market renting, but it will be for as long as tenants are portrayed as second-class citizens, thus allowing public spending to be heavily biased in favour of the reputed moral superiority of a mortgage. A truly sustainable, balanced housing policy would recognise that we may all need different types of housing at different stages in our lives. Moreover, one of the key characteristics of US/UK housing misery is how far up the social ladder it extends. Some of the stories in this book describe the extremes of the housing crisis. But there's a far more commonplace form of housing suffering that now affects millions, dictating where they live and work, consuming vast quantities of their income and stunting the development of their independent adult and family lives.

The State doesn't have to be the sole provider or guarantor of decent affordable homes. But iniquity and volatility make the housing market intrinsically unable to play that role. However, those advocating large-scale public investment in housing must recognise that an accretion of stigma has built up to the point where those under 35s most affected by the current housing crisis may no longer look to the State for help. Some of the arguments for public and council housing have to be re-won, informed by the mixed experiences on both sides of the Atlantic. The simplistic link between poor housing and structural design needs to be broken, but so does institutional uniformity in architecture and management. Advances in building technology mean we can now build better, more energy- efficient homes more quickly without resorting to the one-size-fits all, build 'em high, sell 'em cheap practices of the past. But this can't be done for as long as profit-driven private developers, speculators and landlords are allowed to dominate housing policy, while non-market housing is treated as residual or as the "step-child" of other government initiatives.

Housing in general and public/council housing in particular needs to be part of the political and policy mainstream. The appalling conditions of the first 100 years of the industrial city brought demands for reform backed by rent strikes, protests and direct action. Politicians were compelled to act. Public and council housing, along with some regulation of private renting, were the result. Slums and homelessness have returned with a vengeance to the US and UK, but the political response has been a fatal combination of indifference and exacerbation. Rather than tame the housing market, both US and UK governments have fed it, partly because, despite everything that resulted from sub-prime, they continue to see housing as a form of economic alchemy.

The ideological onslaught from the right against non-market housing alternatives is sometimes echoed from the left by those who conflate public ownership with "State control". Visions of identical blocks running for miles – from the Soviet Union to Chicago – have distorted perceptions of mass public housing for rent. While the problems of such housing have been deliberately exaggerated and exacerbated by those who were always hostile to it, there's one crucial lesson to learn as we think about better, more humane housing policies: scale and numbers matter. Given the magnitude of the problem, only significant sustained government investment can ensure that millions of US and UK citizens can escape a bleak housing future. This has to take the form of insulating a substantial proportion of the housing stock from the vicissitudes of the housing market. But this must not be translated into authoritarian, paternalistic, bureaucratised relationships between public landlords and tenants. The more remote the delivery and administration of day-to-day housing services, the less they work. Good housing management (a necessary if overly-professionalised activity), adequately financed and devolved to local level, has the potential to be a force for social cohesion and solidarity, instead of the frustrating, alienating experience it has too often been.

One of the key arguments for high-quality, publically-owned, readily available rented housing is that it can be a popular alternative to the private market. That's why the US real estate industry and its UK equivalents don't like public/council housing (although as the UK housing crisis deepens, private property interests are increasingly joining the call for direct investment in non-market homes). Almost all of us have an interest in there being enough decent, genuinely-affordable housing for everyone. Only a few have an interest in there not being, but that, as Herbert Marcus argues, is precisely the rationale of housing under capitalism: "The housing crisis doesn't exist because the system isn't working. It exists because that's the way the system works".[196]

The consequences of abandoning our housing fates to the whims of the market are grimly displayed in grotesque form in today's USA, but as Marcuse says, the crisis is endemic. It appears, as J K Galbraith suggested in *The Culture of Contentment*, that the US ruling elite has decided a certain number of victims (tens of

---

[196] For a discussion of why the concept of "housing crisis" is questionable and a lot of other very important issues, see David Madden and Peter Marcuse (2016) *In Defense of Housing*, London, Verso.

millions!) are acceptable so long as North American society can maintain the illusion that private home ownership is the ultimate symbol of free market capitalism. A host of social and political tensions now disfigure the richest nation on earth, directly or indirectly linked to its chronic housing policy failure. Shanty-towns, mass evictions, street homelessness and abandonment are the most obvious, if often ignored, features, but there are more subtly damaging side-effects of the housing malaise. There is a profound sense that many Americans live parallel lives in which housing has become both a dividing wall and a repository for suspicion, fear and anger.

This dynamic is encapsulated by the February 2012 killing of Trayvon Martin because he was in a place he "didn't belong".[197] The case became notorious because it pressed hard on America's sore spots: "race" or, more precisely, the relationships between "whites" and "blacks", colonisation, the Deep South, the legacy of slavery, segregation, poverty, fear, guns, lethal violence and a dysfunctional housing system that is historically racist and continues to reinforce socio-economic and spatial discrimination. The 17-year old died in a place where housing had become an instrument of social and ethnic division. He was shot by George Zimmerman, a security guard in an exclusive gated housing development of the kind that embodies American aspiration, inequality and paranoia.[198] Nearby was a public housing project – the sum of all fears for many Americans – where 483 affordable rented homes had been lost, part of the national onslaught against public housing. This had destabilised the local African-American community. But in an ironic twist, some displaced public housing tenants had been rehoused in private developments that had become empty and devalued since

---

[197] For a detailed account of the background to the Martin killing, see Dan Zak's excellent article "On eve of Trayvon Martin shooting trial, present of Sanford Fla, is shadowed by past", *Washington Post*, 23rd June 2013.
[198] Low S (2003) *Behind the Gates: Life, Security and the Pursuit of Happiness in fortress America*, New York, Routledge.

the 2008 crash. Trayvon was visiting one such family when he met Zimmerman, with tragic consequences.

The Black Lives Matter campaign began with the acquittal of Martin's killer and exploded in another place disturbed by a toxic combination of discriminatory housing practice and racism. Before the killing of Michael Brown in August 2014, Ferguson, Missouri was another anonymous US suburb. But as in the Trayvon Martin case, the fatal shooting of a young black man by someone representing "law and order", exposed some of the latent tensions within US society. From the middle of the 20th century, Ferguson experienced profound demographic movements typical of the recent lifecycle of US cities. Having been an affluent and then "white flight" suburb of St Louis, the area had become home for those displaced from or priced-out of the city.

In 1970, 99 per cent of Ferguson residents were white, in 2010, 70 per cent were black. As low and medium income African-Americans left the inner-city, affluent, predominantly white "millennials" were repopulating it, attracted to a putative urban revival featuring glossy private property developments and "luxury" housing. This "resegregation" of St Louis is a continuation of deliberate policies using housing as a device for social and ethnic engineering. But as Richard Rothstein argues,[199] what happened in Ferguson is typical of the pattern across the US, with the additional historic irony that St Louis is the place where the ritualistic destruction of the nation's public housing began.[200]

The housing and social dynamics of Ferguson and the rest of the US differ from the UK only by degree. The systemic attacks on non-market rented housing, escalating housing costs, resurgent private landlordism, urban displacement and impoverishment and the social isolation of the suburbs are the result of wilful government policies. They pursue the absolute domination of

---

[199] Richard Rothstein, "The Making of Ferguson", *American Prospect*, 13th October 2014.
[200] At Pruitt Igoe in 1972.

private property and individualism over any sense of housing as a civic responsibility.

Ultimately, housing is about politics, but it's a strange anomaly that at a time when millions of US and UK citizens are preoccupied with the struggle to find and keep a decent home, the subject remains at the periphery of the political mainstream. That could be changing, in a way that reflects the peculiar characteristics of each country and compounds the stark dangers for the UK in following US footsteps. The extraordinary surges of support for Bernie Sanders and Jeremy Corbyn reflect deep disillusionment with the political status quo, but so did those for Donald Trump and Nigel Farage/UKIP. Both Sanders and Corbyn have directly highlighted the housing crisis in their manifestos (and both have long track records of supporting grass-roots housing campaigns). Trump and Farage exploited the housing issue by connecting it to anger articulated in resentment targeted at immigrants.

Trump also personifies the fundamental choice that exists between a housing system based on social need or one based on the accumulation of personal wealth. He is the ultimate property tycoon cum politician, a 1% billionaire who buys and sells peoples' homes like second hand cars, and then used his resulting fortune and power to become President of America. He now claims to represent the people who are the victims of the housing system he embodies.

Despite his bogus anti-establishment claims, Trump's appeal is based on the establishment ideology that housing can be reduced to the law of the jungle. This is making the necessity of shelter, once again, a personal quest for survival. This reactionary process has reached a tipping point in the UK and the abyss into which we stare is visible in the US. But it's not too late! The Housing and Planning Act and the whole direction of current policy, threatens to reshape the UK housing landscape in an American image. It is an existential challenge not just to what remains of council housing, but to the entire philosophy it represents. However, while these values have been in retreat for at least three decades, something has changed.

For the first time in a generation, a national political leader has committed to reviving non-market housing. Jeremy Corbyn has been unequivocal in his opposition to the Housing and Planning Act and if he's elected prime minister, has pledged to build one million homes in five years, of which half will be council homes.[201] Whether Corbyn succeeds or not, this reprise of the programme initiated by the post-1945 Labour government reflects a growing consensus in the UK that the housing crisis caused by the market cannot be solved by it.

Jeremy Corbyn, like Bernie Sanders, has linked housing reform to a much broader, transformational shift in public policy. Nothing less will reverse the damage being done to the lives of millions by wanton profiteering in housing. Whatever happens to Messrs Corbyn[202] and Sanders, the pent-up demands for change they've uncorked won't go away. The fight for a real housing alternative is reaching a critical phase. But with the best traditions of the American and British people, it can – and must – be won. The importance of a decent, secure, affordable home to our social and personal lives can't be over-stated. This is currently threatened by forces that want to turn back the clock to a time when the predatory private landlord reigned supreme. Matthew Desmond's conclusion about the US housing crisis has increasing resonance in the UK:

> It can be overwhelming to consider how much happiness has been lost, how many capabilities snuffed out, by the swell of poverty in this land and our collective decision not to provide all our citizens with a stable and decent place to live. (*Evicted*, p300)

Desmond's prescription for solving the US housing crisis is a universal system of housing vouchers. While this would certainly

---

[201] The Labour Party's 2017 election manifesto words this more ambiguously.
[202] At the time of writing, a general election is pending in the UK.

help many poor and desperate Americans, it would only address the symptom, not the cause. Vouchers, or their equivalent, are an indirect public subsidy to private landlords, one that in the UK has reached £9 billion a year in the form of Housing Benefit. That public money and other government subsidies to private property interests, could and should be used for direct investment in top-quality, genuinely affordable, energy-efficient homes preserved in public ownership for future generations. As well as being a false economy, a voucher system linked to the inherent volatility and resulting transience and atomisation of the private rented sector is incompatible with the kind of strong, stable, reciprocal communities that make life better.

The post-war settlement has been unwound more rapidly in respect of housing than in any other aspect of UK public policy. The entire welfare state, including the National Health Service, is currently at risk. The process is reaching a critical point for housing. The spectre of the US model looms – and so does the next economic crash resulting from it. But the sense that the problem is overwhelming and beyond our collective control bolsters the power of those with a vested interest in perpetuating the housing crisis.

We underestimate ourselves! In November 2014, the Rosetta space mission landed a probe the size of a fridge on the surface of a comet travelling through space at a speed of 41,000mph after a ten year journey of four billion miles. Together, we CAN solve the housing crisis!

Last words

The fight for housing justice is important in its own right. But our demands for decent homes for all become more urgent when linked to other campaigns for social equality. This is a period when the fight to save our homes assumes global and historic significance. We stand at a fork in the road between housing that can help us all build good lives, or shatter them. The choice has never been starker. It was eloquently expressed by Eleanor Walden, an NAHT Board member from California, in a message to UK anti-racist campaigners in London on 18th March 2017:

> We stand in solidarity with people in the UK and Europe who resist the rise of xenophobia and racism. Borders do not limit those tendencies. They spread around the world. Now is the time for internationalism. As citizens of the world, we're faced with policies that undermine the health and security of the poor in general and people of colour in particular. We are threatened with the destruction of our rights, homes, health and security. Hate, racism, misogyny and the hardening to the fate of refugees will be the result.

> We cannot allow this. We face a dangerous parallel to the rise of Nazism which is typified by corporatism, militarism and the targeting of a scapegoat population. Truly great societies are built on a foundation of universal principles. Some of these are found in the US constitution – promoting the general welfare and securing the blessings of liberty.

> We must stand in international solidarity with the people around the world who unite against racism and promote the ethics of peace, unity, the human family and hope for our future.

Suggested further reading

Alexander C (2009) *Britain's New Towns; Garden Cities in Sustainable Communities*, Abingdon, Routledge

BrandesGratz R (2015) *We're Still Here Ya Bastards: How the people of New Orleans rebuilt their city*, New York, Nation Books

Bridge G, Butler T and Lees L (2012) *Mixed Communities: Gentrification by stealth?*, Bristol, The Policy Press

Bristol K (2004) *The Pruitt-Igoe Myth in American Architectural History: A Contemporary Reader*, Eggener K (ed), London, Routledge

Bruegmann R (2005) *Sprawl: A Compact History*, Chicago, University of Chicago Press

Darley G (1975) *Villages of Vision: A Study of Strange Utopias*, London, Architectural Press, 2007 edition, Nottingham, Five Leaves Publications

Engels F (1872) *The Housing Question*, Moscow, Progress Publishers

Fishman R (1977) *Urban Utopias in the Twentieth Century: Ebenezer Howard, Frank Lloyd Wright, and Le Corbusier*, Cambridge; MIT Press (1982 edition)

Flint A (2009) *Wrestling with Moses: How Jane Jacobs took on New York's Master Builder and Transformed the American City*, New York, Random House

Garreau J (1991) *Edge City: Life on the New Frontier*, New York, Doubleday

Grindrod J (2013) *Concretopia: A journey around the rebuilding of postwar Britain*, Brecon, Old Street Publishing

Hall P and Ward C (1998) *Sociable Cities: The Legacy of Ebenezer Howard*, Chichester, James Wiley and Sons Ltd

Jacobs J (1961) *The Death and Life of Great American Cities*, London; Pimlico (2000 edition)

Katz P (1994) (ed) *The New Urbanism: Toward an Architecture of Community*, New York, McGraw-Hill

Kostof, S. (1991) *The City Shaped*, New York, Bulfinch Press

Lees L, Slater T and Wyly E (2010) *The Gentrification Reader*, Abingdon, Routledge

Lefebvre H (2003) *Henri Lefebvre: Key Writings* eds. Elde S, Lebas E, Kofman E, London, Continuum

Miller M (2002) *Letchworth: The First Garden City* (2nd edition), Chichester, Phillmore and Co.

Mumford L (1961) *The City in History*, London, Pelican Books

Ravetz A (2001) *Council Housing and Culture: The History of a Social Experiment*, London, Routledge

Simms A (2007) *Tescopoly: How one shop came out on top and why it matters*, London, Constable and Robinson

Theodore N (2002) (eds) *Spaces of Neolibaralism; Urban Regeneration in North America and Western Europe*, Oxford, Blackwall

United Nations (2009) *The Right to Adequate Housing*, Geneva, UN High Commissioner for Human Rights

Index

National Alliance of HUD Tenants
TENANTS UNITED
TO SAVE OUR HOMES

Founded in 1991, NAHT is the first national membership organization of resident groups advocating for 2.1 million lower income families living in government-assisted housing in the US. Through NAHT, tenants have proven that united action can mount an effective campaign to save people's homes.

www.nahtsaveourhomes.wordpress.com
naht@saveourhomes.org
+ 1 617-522-4523

Museum Square protest in DC.

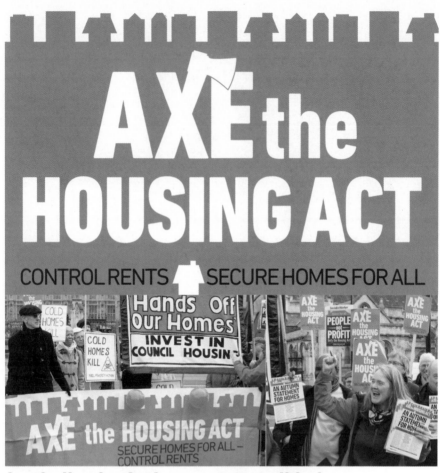

AXE the HOUSING ACT

CONTROL RENTS 🏠 SECURE HOMES FOR ALL

Axe the Housing Act is a non-party political alliance of tenants, trade unionists and housing activists dedicated to opposing the 2016 Housing and Planning Act. Come and join the fight for controlled rent and decent, secure homes for all.

www.axethehousingact.org.uk

info@axethehousingact.org.uk

Tel. +44 (0)7432 098440